Dictionary
of
SEWING
TERMINOLOGY

Linda Carbone

ARCO PUBLISHING COMPANY, INC.
NEW YORK

Published by Arco Publishing Company, Inc.
219 Park Avenue South, New York, N.Y. 10003

Library of Congress Cataloging in Publication Data

Carbone, Linda.
   Dictionary of sewing terminology.

   1. Sewing—Dictionaries.   I. Title.

TT705.C37   646.2'03   77-2559
ISBN 0-668-04039-4 (Library Edition)

ACKNOWLEDGMENTS

My thanks and appreciation are due to the following people for their assistance and encouragement in the preparation of this dictionary: Every student I have ever had for their endless questions, the answers to which are in this book; Lee Louis and Penny Sherred for their enthusiastic support; and of course, my beloved family, Bob, Adrienne, Darlene, Peter, and my mother, all of whom showed great patience when mine had run out!

Linda Carbone
June, 1977

INTRODUCTION

What is a dressmaker? A dressmaker is a creative artist; a person who expresses her own individuality the moment she unwraps fabric, cuts, sews, and finishes a garment to her own special requirements and fashion sense.

This comprehensive *Dictionary of Sewing Terminology* was born because of an obvious need expressed by innumerable students I have had in sewing classes over many years. A typical comment is: "I really do want to be able to sew, but although guide sheets have excellent instructions and illustrations, they frequently use words which I am not sure I fully understand, such as 'stay-stitch,' 'cut on bias,' and 'clean finish.' I need a basic reference book to which I can turn when in doubt."

There are millions of home sewers, students, teachers, and schools in the United States who have the same need of such a book, and it is hoped that this dictionary will provide an easy understanding of the professional sewer's terminology.

A

ABUTTED SEAM

Two cut edges joined together, edge to edge, with an underlay of fabric.

ACCESSORIES

Those parts of wearing apparel which complete the "fashion look," i.e., gloves, shoes, handbag, etc.

ACCESSORY, SEWING MACHINE

See SEWING MACHINE ACCESSORY.

ACCORDION PLEATS

Folds of fabric pressed along entire length of area to resemble the bellows of an accordion.

ACETATE

Fabric term for man-made fiber often used in blends of cotton and rayon, etc. Good draping qualities, elegant feel.

ACRYLIC

Fabric term for man-made lightweight but bulky fiber. Soft, woolen feel. Often blended with other fibers. Used to make knitted and wool-like fabrics.

ADHERE

To firmly attach. To fuse together; i.e., fusible interfacing is joined by heat to facing pieces or to main fabric.

ADHESIVES

Special glues which can be used on leather, trims, and fabrics in place of stitching.

ADJUST

To make minor changes on patterns before cutting fabric.

ADJUSTABLE PATTERN

Pattern selection containing two or more sizes printed on same pattern; for the slightly out of proportion figure sizes; range consecutively, such as 8/10, 10/12, etc. When cutting, use outer cutting lines for larger measurements and inner cutting lines for smaller measurements.

ADJUSTMENT LINES

Double lines printed on a pattern piece indicating where the pattern should be shortened or lengthened, according to body measurements.

AGAINST GRAIN/WITH GRAIN

Fabric reference. When threads feel smooth, running downward, fabric is "with grain"; when threads feel rough, running upward, it is "against grain." Particularly obvious in fake furs, etc.

ALENÇON

Needlepoint lace worked into floral designs on a net background. Pattern is outlined with heavy thread. May be purchased in many widths. Seen on bridal gowns, lingerie, and elegant evening wear.

ALIGN

To match fabric or trim, on exact lines, in stripes, plaids, etc.

A-LINE

Design of dress that begins to flare above waistline then tapers slightly wider at hem. Does not fit snugly at waist or hip. Flattering to figures with heavy hips.

ALLOWANCE

Extra fabric within the garment to accommodate gathers, tucks, shirring, etc.

ALL-PURPOSE FOOT

The part of a sewing machine that holds fabric steady while sewing. Sometimes called "general purpose foot." The foot has two equal length "toes" used for most sewing. *See* FOOT.

ALTERATION

The building or changing of a garment or pattern.

ANGLE

The area at which two points meet, e.g., the point of a collar.

ANGORA

Smooth, soft, silky hair of the angora goat. A natural fiber labeled as wool. Also called mohair.

APEX

The fullest part of a body curve, e.g., the center of the breast, usually the nipple; also the narrow end of a dart.

APPLIQUE

To sew a design of material on to the main fabric. May be sewn by hand or machine. Can be applied with double-faced fusible interfacing or can also be purchased with its own adhesive backing.

APPLY

To join one part to another, such as to apply a button, to apply lace, to apply a zipper, etc.

ARM HOLE

Opening in a garment for the arm to pass through. Line on pattern piece indicating where set-in sleeve is to be sewn to garment. Also called armscye.

ARM LENGTH

Body measurement taken from shoulder bone to elbow, then to wrist with arm slightly bent. Record both lengths. Use as guide when measuring pattern sleeve length.

ARMSCYE

The opening for a sleeve. *See* ARM HOLE.

ARROW

Symbol on pattern pieces. On the seamline, the arrow indicates direction for cutting and stitching. A double-pointed arrow indicates straight grain of fabric on which pattern must lie parallel to selvage edge. Arrow shows direction of pleat fold, tucks, and fold line of pattern.

ARROWHEAD TACK

Hand-worked decorative stitch, triangular shaped, used to reinforce and emphasize pleats, pockets, and slits of garments, giving a custom-tailored look.

ASCOT

A broad neckscarf, tied around the neck so that one end falls over the other.

ASSEMBLE

To gather together necessary pieces of equipment, patterns, notions, etc., needed for sewing.

AWL

See STILETTO.

B

BABIES

See FIGURE TYPE. Figure type for pattern selection for babies is determined according to weight and height. If weight and height vary from pattern sizes, select pattern by weight.

BACKING

Fabric joined to wrong side of garment. Generally used for reinforcement.

BACKSTITCH

A reinforcing stitch used at the beginning or end of a seam by sewing several stitches backwards over the same stitching line. May be done by hand or machine. Also a hand-stitch which appears as machine-stitching on right side of fabric and as overlapped stitching on wrong side.

BACK VIEW

Illustration on back of pattern envelope which shows construction details and design of the back of the garment.

BACK WAIST LENGTH

A measurement taken on the body from the most prominent bone at center back neck down to natural waistline.

BACK WIDTH

Body measurement taken at widest part of back, across shoulder blades to armhole seams.

BACK-WRAP

Skirt style which wraps around the body and is held closed at the back by buttons, ties or hooks at waistline.

BALANCE

Fabric and lines in proportion to figure type. The total look of a wardrobe, when the various elements are equally represented.

BALANCE LINES

The horizontal level on which the crosswise grain of fabric falls at a right angle to lengthwise grain in each garment section. A "T" square is helpful in measuring locations.

BALANCED PLAID

See EVEN PLAID.

BALLPOINT NEEDLE

A machine needle with a rounded point created to slip easily through knit fabrics and synthetics. Used to avoid "pulls" in fabric and to avoid "skipped" stitches (machine stitches which appear unevenly long and short). Size #14 is the average size of this needle.

BALMACAAN

Coat style, loosely fitted.

BAND

Strip placed on garment or accessory to hold together, decorate, or complete a fashion look. May be of ribbon or fabric, cut on bias, or straight of grain.

BARGELLO

A form of needlepoint.

BAR TACK

A hand- or machine-stitch used to reinforce areas of strain, such as ends of buttonholes.

BASIC PATTERN

Pattern printed and altered for correct fit on woven or non-woven fabric or paper. Used to compare with other patterns to make correct pattern adjustments.

BASTE MARK

See BASTE STITCH.

BASTE STITCH/BASTE MARK

A long machine- or hand-stitch made through wrong side of fabric over marking, in contrasting thread, so that stitches appear on right side of fabric. Used for placement of buttonholes, pockets, etc.

BASTING

A temporary stitch used to hold two or more fabric pieces together until permanently sewn. May be done by hand or machine. Prevents fabric from slipping while stitching seams. Helps in matching plaids and for garment fitting. Use longest stitch for machine basting.

BATEAU/BOAT

Neckline shaped around the curve of collar bone.

BATIK

The technique of creating designs on fabric by using a wax and dye method. Originated in Malaya.

BATTING

Matted fibers for use as insulation and underlining in quilts, garments, pillows, etc. May also be used as filling in shoulder pads.

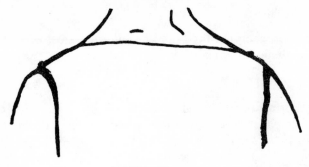

BATEAU

BEADING

1. Open-work trimming through which ribbon may be inserted, usually of lace or embroidery. 2. Narrow lace-like trimming. 3. Material adorned with beads.

BEADING HOOK

A slender instrument used for hand-attaching beads to fabrics.

BEADING NEEDLE

An extra long and slender needle used in sewing beads to fabric.

BEADS

Small, shaped objects with hole opening for needle to pass through. Made of plastic, metal, or other firm materials. Used decoratively. Purchased in packages, or pre-strung by the yard.

BEATER

See POUNDING BLOCK.

BEESWAX

A smooth wax sold at notion counters. Passing thread over the wax gives added strength to thread for sewing on buttons, making hems, etc. Prevents thread from tangling; also smooths surface of iron.

BELL SLEEVE

Full sleeve, wider at bottom edge, shaped like a bell.

BELT

A length of material used to encircle the waist of a garment.

BELT CARRIER

A thread loop or strip of material placed on a garment to support the weight of a belt.

BELTING

Stiffening used as a backing or interlining for belts and in waistbands. Gives more strength and body. Sold by the yard or in packaged "kits."

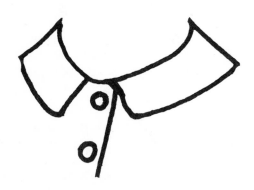

BERMUDA FLAT

See COLLAR. Small collar, flat shaped with pointed ends.

BEVELING

Blending, grading, or layering. To trim all seam allowances within the one seam to different widths. Removes bulk so that seams will lie flat. Eliminates ridges or marks when pressing.

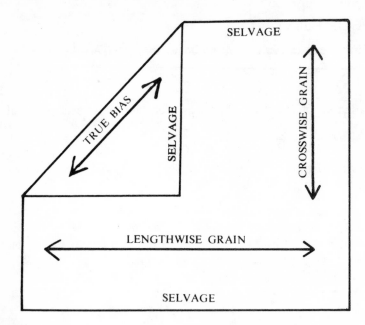

BIAS

A diagonal line that is on neither the lengthwise nor crosswise grain. A "true" bias is the diagonal line formed when the lengthwise grain of fabric is folded to the crosswise grain.

BIAS BINDING/BIAS TAPE

Strips of fabric, cut on the bias, used as a finish or trim. *Double-fold bias tape*: used to encase raw edges to prevent raveling of fabric, it sews easily around curves and has a slightly off-center fold. *Single-fold bias tape*: may be used as a hem finish on very flared skirts, and is also used as decorative trim. Available in various widths and colors.

BIAS DART

See FRENCH DART.

BIAS FACING

Strip of bias-cut fabric or tape, used to finish curved edges.

BIAS STRIPS

Narrow strips of fabric cut on bias, used to finish edges or in areas needing extra ease; also as a trim.

BIKINI

Very brief panty-type undergarment, or a swimsuit with this type of panty.

BINDER

See SEWING MACHINE ACCESSORY. This is a sewing machine accessory used to quickly apply purchased, or self-made, bias binding to an unfinished edge; may be decorative or used to finish raw edges that ravel easily. Straight stitching or zigzag stitching may be used. Seen often on edges of curtains, aprons, etc.

BINDING

See BIAS BINDING and SEAM BINDING.

BIRDSEYE

Fabric description; depicting an all-over design of small, diamond shapes, each having a center dot. Woven into cotton and synthetics. Also seen on piqué fabrics.

BISHOP SLEEVE

Sleeve which is loose to the wrist edge; held together by a band at wrist.

BLANKET BINDING

A 2″ to 3″ folded tape, made on straight grain of fabric used to replace worn bindings on blankets; also used as a decorative trim.

BLANKET STITCH

A decorative edge finish for hand-sewn buttonholes, designs, etc., formed by interlocking stitches closely together.

17

BLAZER

A jacket style, having a notched collar, with one or more button closings.

BLEEDING

The change or loss of color in fabric after washing or dry cleaning.

BLEND

1. A yarn or fabric combining two or more different kinds of fiber, i.e., nylon and cotton. 2. Trimming seam allowances to different widths thereby eliminating bulk or ridges on right side of garments.

BLIND STITCH

A hand-stitch used for hemming which is invisible on right side of fabric. Prepare hem, roll back ¼" of finished edge, taking small stitch on hem side and one stitch on garment side, working in a zigzag manner; may be done by machine using blind hem selector.

BLOCK

To shape a finished product.

BLOCK PRINTING

Hand process of printing fabrics, using shaped blocks of wood or linoleum.

BLOUSE

An article of clothing that ends below the waist, sometimes with fastenings, sleeves, and collar.

BLOUSON

Soft, bloused effect, gathered in at seamline of waist, falling loosely over the waist seam. Seen in dresses and blouses.

BOAT

See BATEAU.

BOBBIN

See SEWING MACHINE ACCESSORY. Machine part under slide plate, filled with thread needed for machine sewing. Thread from bobbin is picked up by top machine thread, thereby forming stitches when sewing. Specific bobbins are required for different brands of machines.

BODICE

The top part of a dress or blouse unit. Pattern pieces indicate "bodice front" and "bodice back."

BODKIN

A heavy needle in different lengths with a blunt point and a large eye; used to draw cord, elastic, tape, etc., through a casing, or for belts, loops, etc. It is sometimes used in forming a thread shank for buttons.

BODY

The stability and extra shaping given to a garment by the fabric itself, or by adding appropriate fabrics, such as interfacings, linings, or underlinings.

BODY MEASUREMENTS

1. Actual measurements of the body considered when purchasing the correct pattern, i.e., bust, waist, hip, back waist length.
2. Measurements on back of pattern envelope that are correct for that specific pattern type and size.

BOLERO

Short jacket, ending above waist.

19

BOLT

Heavy cardboard on which fabric is wrapped and sold by manufacturers. Usually holds up to 20 yards and gives special information: fiber content, washability, width of fabric, etc.

BONDING

Two or more fabrics joined together by an adhesive process to form one fabric. Makes knits and other fabrics easier to handle by giving added body and stability.

BONDING TAPE

See MENDING TAPE.

BONING

See also FEATHER BONING. A flexible piece of bone, plastic, or metal, used on seams and darts that need added support, such as in brassieres, bodice tops, hip areas, and cummerbunds; it is generally fabric covered.

BORDER

An edge finished with commercial trim or self-fabric.

BORDER PRINT

Fabric with prominent design or pattern on one or both selvage edges. Special cutting is required so that design remains at the hemline.

BOUNCE

The recovery of a knit fabric to its original shape after it has been stretched.

BOUND BUTTONHOLE

A buttonhole made with fabric. It is made by using an additional piece of fabric, through a slash in the main fabric, forming "lips," before facing is attached.

BOUND FINISH

A clean, finished edge that may be encased in double-fold bias tape.

BOUTIQUE

Small retail shop, or area in a large store in which accessories and various fashion items are sold.

BOUTONNIERE

Buttonhole.

BOW

Fashion accessory to be worn around the neck and tied into soft folds; it may be of self-fabric, scarves, or ribbon. Also a description of a looped, decorative knot.

BOX PLEAT

Two folds in fabric turned away from each other, with under-folds meeting at center.

BOX PLEAT

BOYS

See FIGURE TYPE. Pattern selection for boys is determined by body measurements, ranging from size 7 to 12, according to height.

BRA CUPS

Molded foam, concave and shaped like the breast; come in several sizes and used as inserts in shaping swimsuit tops and other similar garments.

BRAID

A woven decorative trim. It comes in a variety of fibers, weights, and widths. It may be flat or folded and includes rickrack, soutache.

BROCADE

Rich, woven fabric with raised, interwoven designs on a contrasting surface often with gold or silver threads. Background may be satin, twill, or a combination of weaves.

BROKEN LINES

On pattern pieces, broken lines indicate stitching lines for seams, darts, tucks, pockets, gathers, and trims.

BROWN PAPER

Strips of paper cut from "shopping bags" are an important piece of ironing equipment. When pressing, place strips under folds of darts, hems, pleats, etc. This will avoid ridges and marks appearing on the right side of fabric.

BUCKLE

Closure used with a belt. Size depends upon the width of the belt. Buckles are available in wood, metal, bone, plastic, leather, and pearl and may also be self-fabric covered. Kits are available at notion counters for this purpose.

BURLAP

A coarse, loosely woven fabric usually of 100 percent jute, but sometimes of hemp, or flax. Used for sacking, home decorating, crafts, upholstering, etc.

BUST MEASUREMENT

A measurement taken around the back and across the fullest part of the bust.

BUST POINT

The area on the pattern where the point of bust dart and the waistline dart intersect, indicating exact location of fullest part of bust.

BUTT

To place one edge exactly against another.

BUTTON

A knob or disc used to fasten together different parts of an article, by being attached to one part and passing through a hole or loop of another; also may be used decoratively.

BUTTON FOOT

See SEWING MACHINE ACCESSORY. A sewing machine accessory used for holding a two-hole or four-hole button securely in position while stitching. Using the zigzag stitch on the machine, width is determined by space between holes of button.

BUTTONHOLE

An opening in a garment for a button to pass through; may be finished by hand, machine or by a bound buttonhole.

BUTTONHOLE FOOT

See SEWING MACHINE ACCESSORY. Machine accessory used on sewing machines that have built-in buttonhole feature. The foot has markings for accurate placement of buttonhole.

BUTTONHOLER

See SEWING MACHINE ACCESSORY. A sewing machine accessory that may be purchased to sew buttonholes in accurate length and width; comes with templates in several sizes which control stitch length and style; also makes eyelet-type buttonholes for use in shower curtains, belts, etc. This accessory is used after buttonhole area is completed.

BUTTONHOLE STITCH

Hand-stitch used in making hand-worked buttonholes. Mark for length of opening, machine stitch ⅛ ″ on either side and across both ends. Slash open and work from opening to stitching line with buttonhole twist or matching thread, coated with beeswax for strength. Make close stitches, passing needle through loop before next stitch. At the corners, form a bar tack.

BUTTONHOLE TWIST

A heavy silk thread, used for topstitching areas on coats, suits, and tailored garments.

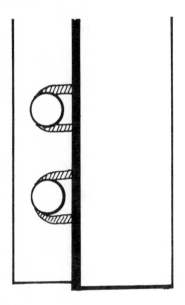

BUTTON LOOP

A carrier made of fabric, leather, etc., to pass over a button to ensure a closure, instead of the conventional buttonhole.

C

CABLE CORD

Soft cord, available in several sizes and lengths, used for tubing and cording.

CAFTAN

A loose, long garment having extra-wide sleeves.

CALENDERING

A finish which gives a smooth, shiny surface to fabric produced by a special process, e.g., glazed cotton.

CALICO

Fabric, usually of cotton and printed with tiny, colorful designs; frequently used when quilting.

CAM, or FASHION DISC

See SEWING MACHINE ACCESSORY. A machine accessory used on sewing machines which have built-in decorative stitches. A variety of designs is available for use in home decorating as well as clothing. Each machine manual gives specific instructions for use.

CAMISOLE

Short, sleeveless under-bodice; generally of lighter weight fabric than main garment. Often joined to skirt and worn under jacket.

26

CANOPY

Fabric draped on frame, usually over a headboard or a four-poster bed.

CANVAS

A firmly woven fabric. Also stiff, open-weave used for needlepoint. Heavier, close-woven canvas may be used for awnings and deck chairs.

CANVAS/HAIR CANVAS

An interfacing used in tailored clothes. A strong, highly resilient fabric made of blends of cotton, wool, and goat hair. Used for shape and support in jackets and coats. Minimizes stretching of garment fabric.

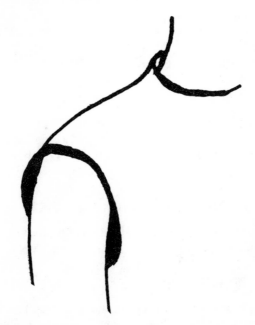

CAP SLEEVE

Short sleeve extending slightly below shoulder line.

CAPE

Loose-fitting, sleeveless outer garment worn over shoulders covering back and arms.

CARDIGAN

Collarless jacket or sweater with center front closings.

CARTRIDGE PLEATS

Extended, unpressed, rounded pleats used generally in home decorating.

CASING

A hem or strip of material with an opening, through which drawstrings or elastic are drawn. Cut-in-one casing in a garment is an extension of fabric folded under, like a hem. Applied casings are bias, straight grain, self fabrics, bias tape, or ribbons that are applied as a separate strip and stitched to garment. Also, opening at curtain top for rod to pass through.

CATCH-STITCH

Hand-worked, secure cross stitch used in areas where edges need to lie flat, generally hems and facings. Working from left to right, take small stitch in hem, then fabric, back to hem, then fabric, and so on to the end.

CENTER FRONT/CENTER BACK LINES

Markings on pattern pieces indicating where garment is to fall at the center of body.

CENTER ZIPPER APPLICATION

Type of closing using a conventional "neckline" zipper, on dresses, skirts, etc., that should have a flat appearance, eliminating bulk. Finished with ¼" top stitching on outside of garment. Use zipper foot for easy application.

CHAIN STITCH

See SEWING MACHINE ACCESSORY. Hand or machine stitch with interlocking loops. Used in making belt carriers, basting, and decorative outline stitching. In machine chain stitching, specific machines have individual instructions.

CHAIN WEIGHTS

Metal links of chain, used mostly in tailoring. Placed in hem, gives added weight to areas of coats or jackets to keep garment hanging evenly.

CHALK

See TAILOR'S CHALK.

CHALK MARKER

A measuring gauge to set skirt lengths. There are three different types available: 1. A rubber bulb filled with chalk-dust, on an adjustable, ruled stand. When the bulb is squeezed, a puff of chalk marks hemline. Can be used without the assistance of another person. 2. A movable bracket placed against skirt; pin is manually inserted at desired length. 3. A marker using a combination of chalk and/or pins.

CHECK

Fabric pattern of squares, similar to checkerboard.

CHEMISE

A loose-fitting shirt-style of dress or blouse.

CHENILLE

Fabric with tufts of pile yarns on flat surface. Used for bed-spreads and robes.

CHEST

A measurement taken around the body: across the back, under the arms and across fullest part of chest.

CHESTERFIELD

Plain coat, with notched collar. Sometimes collar is made of velvet.

CHEVRON

V-shaped, striped design.

CHIC

Original in style and dress.

CHIFFON

Delicate, sheer fabric in plain weave. Usually soft. Also means lightweight, as in chiffon velvet and wool.

CHILDREN

See FIGURE TYPE. Pattern selection is determined by chest measurement and height. Ranging in size from 1 to 6X. These patterns are longer, and the shoulders wider, than "Toddler."

CHUBBIE

See FIGURE TYPE. Patterns designed for the growing girl with more than average weight for her age and height. In sizes 8½ to 14½ "Chubbie," body measurements should be taken and pattern selected according to breast, waist and back waist length.

CIRCULAR KNIT

Knitted fabric in tubular form.

CLAPPER

See POUNDING BLOCK.

CLEAN FINISH

Edge finish on hems, seams, and facings that prevents raveling. There are many methods used: bias binding, edges turned under and stitched, pinking, and French seams.

CLEAR FINISH

See HARD FINISH.

CLIP

A small, straight cut made into the seam allowance, almost to the line of stitching. Helps the seam lie flat around curves, necklines, and at corners.

CLOSURE

Any article which opens or closes a garment, or part thereof (zipper, button, etc.).

CLOTHES BRUSH

Used to raise naps of pile fabrics after pressing, to give a fresh appearance, or to remove marks after pressing. Invaluable for removing lint or threads when applying finishing touches.

COAT/JACKET HANGERS

Short lengths of chain or nylon braid sewn at inside of coat or jacket at back neckline, by which the garment may be hung on a hook, etc.

COAT DRESS

Dress with front closings having coat-like design.

COLLAR

Separate piece of fabric added to neckline, giving a distinctive fashion look. There are several types of collar: 1. *Flat collar*: curves at neckline like the garment neckline. Lies flat against garment, e.g., Peter Pan, Bermuda/Flat, Puritan. 2. *Rolled collar*: rises at neckline seam, then turns down, e.g., notched collar, button-down collar. 3. *Standing collar*: straight, or slightly curved, neckline edge. Stands straight up, e.g., Mandarin, mock turtleneck.

COLLECTION

The exhibition of apparel at fashion shows. Spring and fall are the most popular seasons to show the latest creations to trade and clients.

COLORFAST

Refers to fabric or thread that will not fade or run when cleaned or laundered.

CONSTRUCTION MARKINGS

Symbols printed on a pattern indicating buttonhole placement, folds, darts, pockets, etc. Made in the form of dots, squares, triangles, lines, crosses, etc., each has a specific purpose, and should be transferred to fabric by means of dressmaker's carbon (tracing paper), tailor's tacks and/or bastings.

CONTINUOUS PLACKET

A strip of fabric stitched to an unseamed area from one opening to another and finished by hand or machine. Seen generally on shirt cuffs.

CONTOUR

Shape of body curves. Darts of contour shape, fitting into curve of body.

CONTOUR DART

A stitched fold of fabric that fits at waistline and tapers to a point at both ends.

CONTRASTING

The difference of color in thread, fabric or shadings, such as white basting thread on dark fabric.

CONTROLLED FULLNESS

Amount of gathering necessary on a seam, enabling it to fit into a shorter seam edge.

CONVERTIBLE

Type of collar with small lapels which can be worn open or closed at neck.

CORDED BUTTONHOLE

Bound buttonhole that has cable cord encased between lips of fabric. On hand-worked buttonholes, buttonhole twist thread is placed under worked stitches. It gives a raised effect when completed.

CORDED TUBING

Cord enclosed in bias-cut strips of fabric. Corded tubing may be used to make fasteners, such as loops and frogs.

CORDING

Cord covered with bias-cut fabric strips so that seam allowances of fabric are to the outside, allowing them to be stitched into garment seams. Seen on corded bound buttonholes, at waistlines and on other garment areas.

CORDUROY

Fabric that has raised cut yarns, and has high and low surfaces called "wales." Considered a "with nap" fabric.

33

CORRECTION DART

A fold on a fitting muslin from one seam to another, or from seam to the point of dart. Used to remove fullness. Repeat fold on pattern piece before cutting garment fabric.

COTTON

Natural fibers obtained from the cotton plant, spun into yarn, then woven into fabrics. Strong, durable, and absorbent. Excellent for summer wear.

COUCHING

An embroidery stitch, using heavy thread or cord.

COURSES

Rows of loops which are crosswise in knit fabric.

COUTURIER

Male designer, head of a dressmaking house.

COUTURIERE

Woman designer and dressmaker.

COWL

A softly draped neckline.

CRAVAT

Folded or tied necktie, having ends tucked inside garment.

CREASE

1. Line or mark made when pressing a fold of fabric. 2. Line or mark which may result on fabric when manufacturer rolls folded fabric on bolt.

CREASE RESISTANT/WRINKLE RESISTANT

Fabric finish that reduces the tendency to wrinkle or crease.

CREPE

Fabric with a crinkled, pebbly surface. May be of wool, silk, or synthetics in a combination of different weights.

CREPE DE CHINE

A soft, fine silk or rayon fabric with very slight irregularities of surface.

CREW

Round neckline that firmly hugs the throat, usually of stretchable fabric.

CREWEL

An embroidered, decorative design, using a hand needle and wool yarn.

CRINOLINE

1. Coarse, stiff fabric used to give body and firmness to belts, drapery headings, etc. 2. A fashion look for women—a full-skirted dress worn over stiffened petticoat over a hooped frame.

CROCHETING

A method of making fabric by hand. A hook is used to knot yarns into series of joined loops.

CROSS STITCH

A hand embroidery stitch forming an "X" on right side of fabric.

CROSSWISE GRAIN

See WOOF. Direction of threads in fabric that run from selvage to selvage.

CROTCH

Body measurement taken when making pants, jumpsuits, bathing suits, etc. Measurement is taken when sitting, from side waist to seat of chair. Crotch depth on pattern back should be body measurement plus ½"-¾" for ease of movement.

CROW'S FOOT

Thread design, triangular-shaped, used as a stay, at stress ends of pleats or pockets.

CUFF

Additional fabric added to wrist edge of sleeve, finished, then turned up, or buttoned.

CULOTTE

Trouser-like garment, designed to simulate skirt with flaring leg parts. *See* GAUCHO.

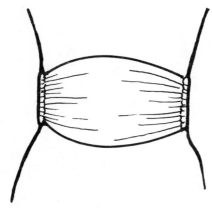

CUMMERBUND

A belt that is gathered and fitted on waist, extending up toward rib cage of body. May be of fabric, ribbon, leather, etc. It is held in position with strips of boning (feather boning).

CURVED RULER

A specially designed ruler used as a guide in drawing curves and in pattern alteration.

CUSHION

See EMERY CUSHION or PIN CUSHION.

CUSTOM FINISH

Perfect fit and construction in garments and home decorating.

CUT-IN-ONE

More than one section of garment cut in one piece, such as bodice and sleeve together, or facing and bodice together.

CUTTING

The long, firm, steady slashes into a fabric. Use dressmaker's shears, never pinking shears, when cutting. Keep one hand flat on fabric to prevent shifting of pattern or fabric.

CUTTING BOARD

Lightweight, but firm, cardboard, that opens flat with inch-square markings for measuring and cutting fabric accurately.

CUTTING LAYOUT

Diagrams on sewing guide sheet, inside pattern envelope, showing pattern layout of view you are making, size of pattern, and width of fabric. View shows selvage edges, fold of fabric, and placement of pattern for fabric, linings, and interfacings. Pin *all* pattern pieces in place before cutting, to ensure all pieces are allowed for.

CUTTING LINE

Heavy, dark line at pattern edge. Also, lines on patterns for cutting different views, such as the short sleeve cutting line on a long sleeve pattern piece.

D

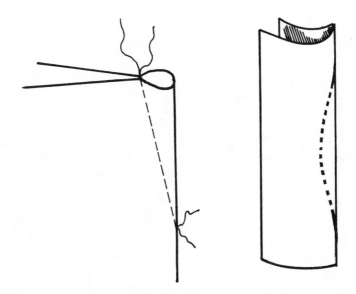

DART

Stitched fold of fabric tapering to a point at one or both ends, used in shaping fabric around curves of body. Darts should be stitched from wide end to point.

DART SEAM

Seam from hemline to bust, tapering up to a point.

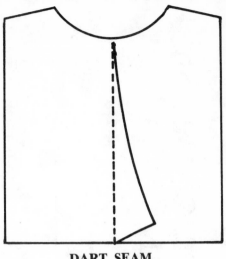

DART SEAM

DART TUCK

Stitched fold of fabric, the reverse of a dart, with wide end forming fullness within garment. Also called "release dart."

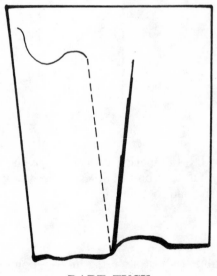

DART TUCK

DECOLLETE

Low-cut neckline, exposing cleavage of bosom, or neck and back, as in formal wear.

DECORATIVE STITCHING

Stitches made by hand or machine to emphasize or decorate an article. Some machines have built-in designs which can be applied by simply changing a dial, e.g., satin stitch, feather stitch, etc.

DENIER

The determined weight of yarn or fibers.

DENIM

Strong, washable twill weave fabric made with colored warp and white filling. Usually made of cotton, but can be purchased in blends. Mostly used for sportswear.

DESIGN ALLOWANCE

Extra ease which designer has added to pattern to permit tucks, gathers, and bloused effects for different fashion looks.

DESIGNER PATTERN

The special pattern with extra details complementing the latest fashion, custom touch, and originality in design. Famous designers have given their creative talents and individuality to these designer patterns.

DETACHABLE COLLAR

Completely finished collar section, bound at neck edge. May be basted to neck edge for easy removal when laundering.

DIAGONAL

The distinct pattern of stripes or design that runs on an angle from one selvage to another. Also bias of fabric.

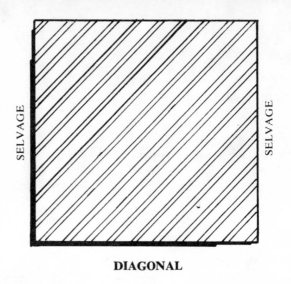

DIAGONAL

DIAGONAL BASTING

A hand stitch used to hold together several layers of fabric during garment construction, such as under-linings to garment section. Helps in handling fabrics while pressing, also during garment fitting.

DIAPHRAGM

A measurement taken around the body between bust and waist-line.

DICKEY

Small, detachable shirt front, to be worn under a garment for a fashion look.

DIRECT DYES

The addition of salt to dyes in order to penetrate fabric.

DIRECT PRINTING/ROLLER PRINTING

An engraved rolling process that transfers color or design to fabric on the right side.

DIRECTIONAL FABRIC

Because of its finish, print, design or weave, such a fabric must be laid out for cutting in one direction only. Considered "with nap," e.g., velvet, one-way designs, satins, etc.

DIRECTIONAL STITCHES

The direction in which stay-stitching and seamlines are to be stitched. It is "with the grain" to prevent excess stretching of fabric.

DIRNDL

Garment fully gathered at waistline.

DOLMAN

Sleeve; set into very deep armhole, cut-in-one and tapering towards wrist.

DONEGAL

Fabric with colorful spots or slubs woven in intervals. Considered a tweed, originating in Ireland. At one time only wool was considered Donegal; now, any tweed, in any fabric may be so named.

DOT MARKER

Long, metal gadget used to transfer dot markings on pattern to fabric by inserting tracing paper between wrong sides of garment, placing marker base beneath both fabric and paper, upper part of marker arm above pattern and pressing sharply on knob. Marks will be neatly transferred.

DOTS

Construction markings on pattern piece as an aid in matching seamlines, pockets, etc. Each should be tailor-tacked with constrasting color thread.

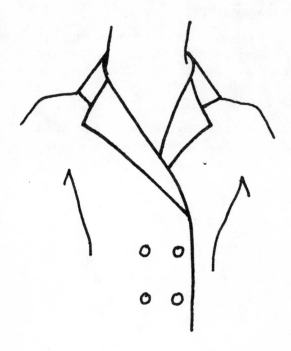

DOUBLE-BREASTED

Front closing on garment overlapping enough to allow two vertical rows of buttons.

DOUBLE-FACED

Term describing fabric which can be used on either side.

DOUBLE-KNIT

Fabric knitted on two sets of needles producing double thickness of fabric. Has excellent shape-retention. Made of variety of fibers and blends. Weights vary from light to heavy.

DRAPE

The way in which fabric falls easily and gracefully; a soft fold. May be controlled by gathers or pleats.

DRAWN WORK

Decorative open thread work on fabric in which threads are drawn out and remaining threads secured in close bunches. Also called hem stitching when hem is turned up first. Seen on tablecloths and place mats, as well as finely made clothes.

DRESS

An article of clothing that falls from the shoulders, with arm openings, ending at length desired.

DRESS FORM

A form which may be shaped to duplicate body measurements. It is helpful in fitting and altering a garment, and excellent for creating new styles and draping. Made of various materials, such as foam, mesh, and fabric-covered batting. All types should have a sturdy base and be adjustable to body measurements.

DRESSMAKER

A seamstress; creative artist; a person who expresses her own individuality the moment she unwraps fabric, cuts, sews, and finishes a garment to her own special requirements and fashion sense.

DRESSMAKER'S CARBON

See TRACING PAPER.

DRESSMAKER'S GAUGE

A small, handy marking tool with a straight edge for marking tucks and pleats and a scalloped edge for making rounded edges.

DRILL CLOTH

Durable cotton or linen twill fabric; generally used for work clothes. Comes in various weights.

45

DRIP DRY

Description of fabrics which, after washing and without wringing, are hung to drip until dry. A garment dried in this manner has very few wrinkles and requires little or no ironing.

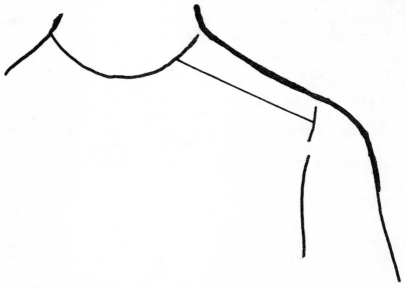

DROP SHOULDER, or FORWARD SHOULDER

A shoulder seam located below normal shoulder line.

DUCK

Heavy, tightly woven cotton fabric in different weights. The most durable fabric for outside furniture.

DUPLEX PRINTING

Process of printing design on front and back of fabric in two operations.

DURABLE PRESS

The wash and wear finish of fabrics. Chemical and heat setting processes give fabrics continued resistance to wrinkles through repeated washings.

DYE

To apply color to fabric, yarn, thread, or any fiber.

DYE-LOT

Fabrics or threads dyed in the same vat at the factory. When reordering fabric, thread, or yarn there is no guarantee of receiving an *exact* match, since the new batch may have been dyed in a different vat, although using the same color.

E

EASE

The even distribution of fullness in fabric without gathers or tucks when one larger seam is joined to a smaller one. This ease provides shaping to areas such as armholes, princess lines, shoulder seams, etc.

EASE ALLOWANCE

An added allowance over body measurements given on pattern. This extra allowance gives needed room in garment for comfort and movement. Without it, the garment would be tight and unattractive.

EASE IN

To fit a larger section into a smaller area of garment accurately without puckers, gathers, or tucks.

EASE STITCHING

Lines of stitching shown on pattern piece used to control fullness, as in sleeve caps. Larger stitching than usual should be placed through one layer of fabric on seamline, then pull up threads from both ends to distribute fullness evenly. Sometimes two rows of stitching are required.

EDGE FINISH

Any finish applied to raw edge, e.g., binding, zigzagging, stitching, overcasting, pinking, etc.

EDGE STITCH

Stitch placed very close to folded edge of garment; used as finish on hems and facings.

EDGE STITCHER

See SEWING MACHINE ACCESSORY. A machine accessory with many and varied uses. Enables stitching accurately on edges of seams, laces, tucks, etc. Lace may be applied and stitched with a tuck in one operation.

EDGING

Novelty, decorative trim such as ribbon, lace, or braid; may be used to finish hem or as a trim on any area of garment.

EDWARDIAN

Garment style taken from Edwardian England; princess line in design, fitted with stand-up collar.

ELASTIC

Rubber material sold in many widths and lengths, which stretches and returns to original shape when released. Used in areas which need closeness of fit without other fasteners. Several types are available: lingerie elastic for undergarments; plush and webbing for girdles; chlorine-resistant for swimsuits; no-roll for waistbands.

ELASTIC THREAD

See THREAD.

EMBOSSED

Raised surface designs on fabric, produced by passing fabric through hot engraved rollers.

EMBROIDERY

Any decorative design on fabric made by using needle and thread. May be done by hand or machine.

EMBROIDERY FLOSS

A form of thread made of six-strand cotton or silk in a complete range of colors. Used for decorative embroidery done by hand.

EMBROIDERY HOOP

Frame with two circular parts fitting snugly over each other with a spring closing. Used to hold a section of fabric firmly in place while sewing. Some are cork-lined and come in various sizes of wood, metal, or plastic.

EMERY CUSHION

A small bag filled with an abrasive powder. Used to sharpen and remove rust from needles and pins. Sometimes attached to larger pincushions. Also called "strawberry."

EMPIRE

Dress style having a high waistline, loose fitting, straight skirt. French Empire period styling.

ENCLOSED SEAM

Any seam concealed by two layers of garment fabric, e.g., French seam.

ENSEMBLE

A complete outfit or costume, such as coat and dress.

EPAULET

Shoulder trim, consisting of a band secured with a button.

EVEN BASTING

Temporary hand stitches that are made ¼″ long and ¼″ apart. Used in areas that need close control, such as curved seams and eased sections, before being permanently stitched.

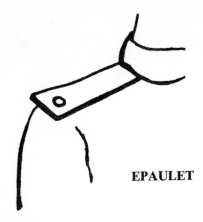

EPAULET

EVEN FEED FOOT

See SEWING MACHINE ACCESSORY. A machine accessory that may be purchased for different models of machines. Exceptional when stitching "hard-to-sew" fabrics, such as velvet, plaid, leather. Sews smoothly; perfect for matching plaids.

EVEN PLAID/BALANCED PLAID

The plaid pattern of fabric that is exactly the same on both sides of center design in both up and down, and left to right directions.

EXPANDED PATTERN

A half pattern that has been duplicated to form one whole pattern piece, such as a complete front or back. Recommended for use with stripes, plaid and matching fabrics.

EXTENDED FACING

A facing that is cut as one with garment piece. When folded back inside garment, folded edge becomes finished edge.

EXTENDED SHOULDER

Shoulder seam which extends below normal sleeve seam. Usually made with long or three-quarter sleeves.

EXPOSED ZIPPER

Type of closing where complete coils of zipper are visible. Generally placed on garment in an unseamed area. Seen often on tops or sweaters of stretchable fabrics.

EXTENSION

Additional fabric extended beyond the edge of a seam or center marking.

EYELET

A small, round hole in fabric, finished by hand or with metal ring. Used for holding prong of a buckle, lacing effects with tubing, ribbon, leather, etc. Metal eyelets are available in kits or packaged with an eyelet punch, and come in many sizes. The larger sizes are called "grommets." *Also:* a fabric. "Eyelet" fabric has open-punched, machine-finished patterns. Floral motifs are most common.

F

FABRIC

Any cloth or fibers or yarns that are knitted, woven, bonded, laminated, or braided. May be manufactured by machine or hand in many lengths and widths. Also referred to as "goods" or "material."

FABRIC FINISH

A process applied to fabric which affects its appearance or performance.

FABRIC WIDTH

Distance from selvage to selvage across width of fabric. Yardage requirements are figured for the most common fabric widths on back of pattern envelope. Most common widths are: 36", 45", 54", and 60".

FACE

The right side of fabric. The more attractive side because of finish or weave.

FACING

A piece of fabric, bias or fitted, applied to necklines, armholes, etc., that turns to underside to finish an edge. Generally, facings are of the same fabric as the garment.

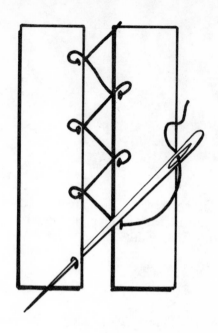

FAGOTING

Trim or stitches that are placed between seams for a decorative look. May be handmade or purchased and is often seen on lingerie.

FAKE FUR

Fabric which simulates animal fur.

FASHION DISC/CAM

See SEWING MACHINE ACCESSORY, under CAM. Interchangeable parts on sewing machine that produce attractive, decorative stitches. Each machine requires its own disc or cam. A few are: zigzag stitching, blind hem, scallops, arrowhead.

FASHION FABRIC

A garment's outer fabric as opposed to linings, etc.

FASTENERS

Garment closures—hooks, snaps, buttons, etc., that open and close a garment.

FASTENING STITCH

Hand-sewing stitch used at the beginning or end of a row of stitching to secure thread.

FAVORING

Rolling one garment section slightly over another at an enclosed seam area to conceal seam. As in tailoring, on a collar.

FEATHER BONING

See BONING.

FEATHER STITCH

Hand embroidery, or machine decorative stitch. Also used as a decorative stretch stitch on undergarments to strengthen seams.

FEED DOG

On a sewing machine, the feed dog is directly under presser foot appearing either as metal teeth or rubber strips. The function of the feed dog is to propel fabric forward or backward as machine is sewing.

FELLING

A hand-stitch used in fine tailoring to attach undercollar to upper collar or coat. A fine, even, firm stitch, used mostly on men's wear.

FELT

A non-woven fabric. Generally comes in 72″ widths. Does not ravel and needs no finish. Used in millinery, fashions, home decorating, and crafts.

FIBER DYEING

A process of adding dye to fibers before they are made into yarn for fabrics or thread.

FIBERS

Substances used to form the yarns or fabric. May be natural or man-made, e.g. wool, cotton—natural; rayon, triacetate—man-made.

FIGURE TYPES

In pattern selection there are various groups of sizes, according to body dimensions. These are figure types. Age is not a factor, body measurements are. Size is determined by horizontal measurements around the body. Ease allowance is included in each pattern. If you are smaller boned and measurements fall between two sizes, choose the smaller size; if you are larger boned, choose larger size. The bust measurement is the most important. Special patterns are "proportioned size" which can be used for figures of different heights. "Adjustable patterns" are for the not-so-perfect figure. Lines on these patterns have two or more sizes for cutting and marking. Refer to each figure type:

BABIES	MATERNITY
BOYS	MEN
CHILDREN	MISS
CHUBBIE	MISS PETITE
GIRLS	TEEN BOYS
HALF-SIZE	TODDLER
JUNIOR	YOUNG JUNIOR TEEN
JUNIOR PETITE	WOMEN

FILLING

The crosswise yarn in fabric. Also referred to as "weft" or "woof."

FINDINGS

Materials used to reinforce and construct a garment, such as padding, interfacing, etc.

FINGER GUARD

See SEWING MACHINE ACCESSORY. An accessory used on sewing machines to safely protect the fingers from the needle. Excellent for the blind and for young students.

FINGER PRESS

Pressing in small areas, by creasing with the fingers.

FINISH

Sewing techniques used to finish raw edges of seams, facings, hems, necklines, etc. Finishing is machine or hand-done. May be by binding, pinking, stitching.

FITTING

Adjustment of garment or pattern to fit an individual figure.

FLANNEL

Soft fabric, loosely woven with slightly fuzzy nap, of cotton or wool. Cottons are used for sleepwear or shirts; wool is used for dresses, coats, suits, etc.

FLAP

Shaped fabric that hangs loosely and is attached at one edge. Generally found over pockets.

FLARE

The part of garment that spreads out and widens at lower edge.

FLAT CONSTRUCTION

A method of stitching garment sections together by adding sleeves before underarm and side seams are stitched.

FLAT FELL SEAM

A double-stitched seam giving a finished look on both sides of garment; used on tailored clothes and sportswear.

FLOCKING

The application of short fibers which are stuck to fabric with adhesive, thereby creating a raised design.

FLOUNCE

An additional circular, gathered, or pleated length of fabric applied to the bottom of skirts, slipcovers or curtains.

FLY PLACKET

Fabric used as a lap-over, concealing a garment closing, such as zippers or buttons; found on men's pants.

FOLD-LINE

Solid line indicated on pattern piece where fabric is to be folded back and finished. This line should be baste-marked for easy reference when pattern is removed from fabric.

FOOT

See SEWING MACHINE ACCESSORY. Machine part used to hold fabric in position while sewing. Many types are available, making a sewing project easier to handle.

FOR STRETCH KNITS ONLY

Pattern selection to be used with very stretchable, unbonded knit fabrics only. Fabric must stretch around the body for a close fit. Ease allowance is less than in patterns required for woven fabrics or firm knits.

FORWARD SHOULDER

See DROP SHOULDER.

FOUNDATION CANVAS

See CANVAS.

FRENCH CUFF

Cuff on sleeve that is twice the width of finished cuff, folded up at wrist, having four buttonholes for cuff links.

FRENCH CURVE

A drawing tool used as a guide for marking short, curved sections. *See* CURVED RULER.

FRENCH DART/BIAS DART

Folded dart, stitched on bias rather than on lengthwise or crosswise grain.

FRENCH KNOT

Decorative hand-stitch used mostly in embroidery. Thread is wound around the needle which is brought down into the fabric, thereby forming a small dot.

FRENCH SEAM

Enclosed finished seam used on sheer and lightweight fabrics that ravel easily.

FRENCH TACK

An extension of thread as a fastening, holding two pieces of garment sections together loosely. For attaching lining to coat at hemline.

FRINGE

Edge finish that is formed by unraveling a cut edge of fabric or loose yarns that are then knotted and applied to section of garment. May be purchased by the piece or hand done.

FROG

A decorative closing formed by looping braid, binding, or cording into curves joined together. Associated with Oriental design, they are made in pairs, one ending with a loop, the other ending with a button.

FRONT WAIST LENGTH

Body measurement taken from base of neck to waist.

FUNNEL COLLAR

Raised neckline flaring outward at top.

FURRIER'S COLD TAPE

A special tape applied to edges or darts on fur, as a reinforcement before seams are sewed.

FUSIBLE ADHESIVES, or WEB

Fiber mesh that secures hems and appliqués by placing mesh between two layers of fabric and applying pressure and the heat of an iron.

FUSING TAPE

See MENDING TAPE.

G

GABARDINE

Firm fabric of cotton and blends of wool, polyester, or rayon, of twill weave, with steep, diagonal lines on face of fabric.

GATHERING FOOT

See SEWING MACHINE ACCESSORY. This accessory on sewing machine can be used for evenly spaced shirring for curtains and clothes.

GATHERING LINES

Short, broken lines on pattern seamline, showing that a larger area must be drawn up to fit into a smaller area, forming soft folds. Machine or hand basting stitches may be used.

GAUCHO

See CULOTTE.

GAUGE

Number of stitches per inch in knitted materials and hosiery. The higher the gauge number the closer and finer the knit. Also, small ruler. *See* SEWING GAUGE.

GAUZE

Thin, sheer, woven fabric, usually of cotton, similar to cheese-cloth.

GENERAL PURPOSE FOOT

See SEWING MACHINE ACCESSORY. Foot on sewing machine with two equal length toes with wide space between them to accept zigzag stitching. Also used for straight stitching when alternating between straight and zigzag. General purpose throat plate must be used.

GIMP

Heavy thread used for strength. Also an upholstery trim.

GINGHAM

Plain weave cotton of medium weight, in checks, plaids, or stripes.

GIRLS

See FIGURE TYPE. Pattern selection. Generally sizes 7 to 14; for the girl who has not yet begun to develop, usually in heights of 4'2" to 5'1". Measurements taken around body will determine proper pattern size.

GIRTH

Measurement taken around the body.

GLAZING

Process of finishing fabric, adding luster and sheen, such as in chintz or everglaze cotton.

GLOVER'S NEEDLE

A three-corner-pointed needle for sewing leather and fur.

GORE

Section of garment that is narrower at top, wider at bottom and is usually on skirts.

GORGE LINE

Diagonal seam, joining the end of collar to lapel.

GRADING

See BEVELING.

GRAIN

The direction of fabric threads, lengthwise or crosswise. Threads that run up and down the length, or parallel to selvage, are lengthwise. Threads running across fabric, between selvages are crosswise. Fabric is "on grain" when these two threads cross each other at perfect right angles. Also called "true grain."

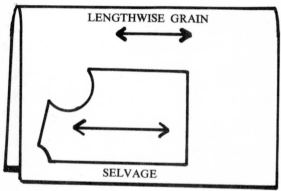

GRAIN LINE

Heavy, solid line on pattern pieces with arrows at either end indicating the direction of grain of fabric. Place this line parallel to fabric selvage along lengthwise grain. Both arrows should be the same distance from fabric edge.

GRAY GOODS (GREIGE)

Fabric that is unbleached, undyed, or unfinished. Also color describing fabric that is between gray and beige.

GROMMETS

See EYELET.

GROSGRAIN

Firm, closely woven ribbon or fabric with pronounced crosswise ribs. Used as trim, and sometimes as facing at waistline.

64

GUIDE SHEET

Printed instruction sheet, included in pattern envelope, giving information on cutting, marking, and complete construction of each pattern view shown on pattern envelope.

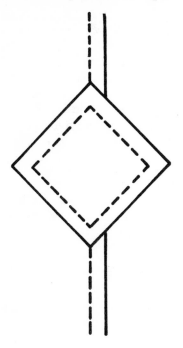

GUSSET

A matching fabric piece inserted in underarm or crotch area of garment to give added ease and comfort.

H

HAIR CANVAS

See CANVAS. Closely woven fabric blended primarily with the hair of goats. Used mainly as interfacing in tailored garments, such as coats and suits.

HAIR CLOTH

A wiry, sturdy interfacing fabric made of horsehair and strong cotton fibers. Used in men's tailoring and sewed over canvas as extra reinforcement.

HALF BACKSTITCH

Hand-stitch used in hard-to-reach areas and for hand topstitching. Top stitches are evenly spaced ⅛" apart; bottom stitches overlap each other.

HALF-SIZE

See FIGURE TYPE. Pattern selection for the shorter, fully developed figure with a shorter back waist length and larger waistline than other figure types.

HALTER

Backless bodice with neckline band held together with closures or tied. Sometimes front part is joined to waist or tied at back.

HAM

See TAILOR'S HAM.

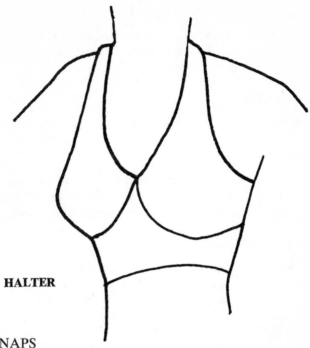

HALTER

HAMMER SNAPS

Fasteners made of metal with plain, round heads or a variety of decorative heads. These two-part snaps withstand hard wear and are ideal for children's clothes. Sold in packages with applicator.

HAND

The feel, drape, and handling of fabric.

HAND-ROLLED HEM

Fine, hand-finished hem formed by rolling raw edges of fabric between fingers and sewing small stitches close together by hand. Seen on scarves, sheer fabrics, and lingerie.

HAND-WORKED BUTTONHOLES

Opening on garment for button to pass through that is made on delicate fabrics and tailored clothes. *See* BUTTONHOLE STITCH.

HARD FINISH/CLEAR FINISH

Surface of fabric that is smooth and flat, has no nap, or may have had nap that has been sheared. Weave is clearly visible and generally of woven fabric.

HEADING

Area above a casing, pleats, or gathers, as at top edge of curtains.

HEM

Finished edge formed by folding back a raw edge and stitching in place by hand or machine. Each method of stitching is determined by depth of hem, garment type, and fabric.

HEM FACING

Extra facing or false hem on skirts and draperies. When a hem is turned down for added length, hem facing gives a finished look to the underside. May be self-fabric or purchased.

HEM GAUGE/HEM AID

A measuring device with markings for various hem depths. Hems can be measured, turned, and pressed in one step.

HEMLINE

Marking on pattern indicating finished edge of garment and depth of hem to be finished. Generally the wider the flare of garment, the narrower the depth of hem.

HEMMER

See SEWING MACHINE ACCESSORY. Special foot for sewing machine designed to turn and stitch narrow hems quickly, without pinning or basting. Excellent for ruffle finishes, scarves, lingerie.

HEMMING STITCH

Hand hemstitch for hems that have been folded and pressed in position or on bound edges. Tiny stitch is taken on garment then diagonally through edge of hem, spacing stitches ¼″ apart, continuing until hem is completely finished.

HEMSTITCHING

See DRAWN WORK.

HERRINGBONE

Fabric with irregular twill weave giving zigzag effect.

HIGH-COUNT FABRIC

Any fabric that is woven closely together.

HIP

Body measurement taken around the hip, 9″ below waist for Miss, Women, and Junior figure types. 7″ below waist for half-size, Junior Petite and Young Junior Teen.

HIP HUGGER

Style of pants, shorts or skirts in which garment starts 2″-3″ below waist and extends downwards.

HOMESPUN

Plain weave wool or cotton fabric; looks hand-loomed; rather thick and heavyweight.

HONG KONG FINISH

A method of finishing in which a bias strip of fabric or binding is stitched to raw edge, turned over edge, and stitched in seamline formed by joined strip. Seen in tailored garments on seams and hems.

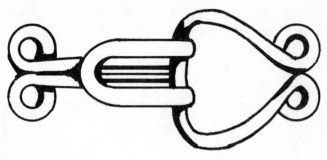

HOOKS and EYES

Metal fasteners that come in a variety of designs. Standard types have two parts—one with hook-shaped end, the other half-moon-shaped, to be sewn separately to each side of garment. Used at neck edges, sleeve bottoms, etc. Sizes range from small to large. Extra large sizes are covered with corded fibers to match coats, furs, etc. Specially shaped adjustable closures are made for waist-bands.

HOOP

See EMBROIDERY HOOP.

HORIZONTAL

The direction across or around the body.

HORSEHAIR BRAID

See HEM. Stiff, woven braid in various widths used in hemming the edge of lightweight, flare skirts, and lace garments to give added support.

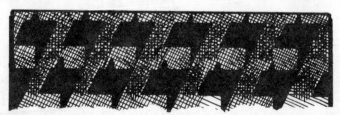

HOUNDSTOOTH

Fabric with four-pointed star check design.

I

ILLUSION

Very fine, sheer tulle, net, or maline fabric, mainly used for bridal veils and dresses.

INSEAM

The seam from crotch to hem on pants, culottes, or any garment with leg parts.

INSERTION

A straight piece of lace or banding set into a garment giving it a decorative look.

INSET

A piece of fabric that has been inserted into a garment for better fit or used decoratively.

INTERFACING

Firm fabric or fusible iron-on materials placed between two layers of garment fabric giving added body, strength, and shape, e.g., in collars, cuffs, waistbands.

INTERLINING

A fabric cut the same as main fabric, of suitable weight, placed between lining and garment, giving added warmth or bulk. Used in coats, jackets, ski wear; in lined draperies, to prevent light coming through and fading fabric; in bedspreads to give extra body. Materials are made up of soft textures of cotton or blends.

INTERSECT

Seams that cross one another at specific areas such as waistline, shoulder line, etc.; when joining sections together they must match perfectly.

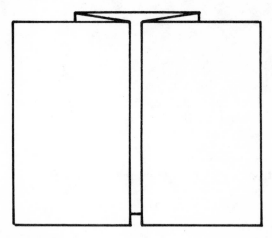

INVERTED PLEAT

See PLEAT. Two pleats that meet at center when turned toward each other.

INVISIBLE ZIPPER APPLICATION

Type of closing on garment where the look of a continuous seam is desired and the zipper is completely hidden by using an invisible zipper. Must be used with a special machine foot. *See* INVISIBLE ZIPPER FOOT.

INVISIBLE ZIPPER FOOT

See SEWING MACHINE ACCESSORY. Special accessory for sewing machine used for applying an invisible zipper. Foot has two "tunnel"-shaped openings on bottom enabling coils of zipper to glide through. When zipper is completed on garment its appearance is of an enclosed seam. This foot may be purchased in several heights for various machines.

IRON

An electrified tool used for pressing and ironing clothes and other items. Most useful is a combination steam and dry iron. Irons with spray attachments provide the extra moisture needed for pressing and tailoring.

IRONING BOARD

A flat, narrow table approximately 54" in length with legs for support. For use in ironing and pressing garments and other items. It should be adjustable to different heights and be well padded.

J

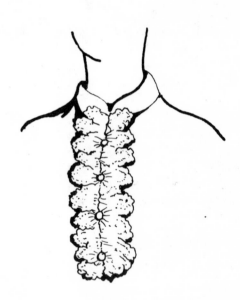

JABOT

Full ruffle down front of bodice that is fastened at neck.

JACKET

Short coat, fitted or unfitted, with sleeves; to be worn over another garment.

JACQUARD

Fabrics woven on special looms creating an intricate and elaborate pattern, e.g., brocades and tapestries.

JERKIN

Short, sleeveless jacket or vest that pulls on over the head.

JERSEY

Smooth, plain-knitted fabric, usually of rayon or synthetic blends, having excellent draping qualities.

JEWEL

Round neckline without collar, at base of neck.

JOININGS

When one section of garment is joined to another, such as yoke to bodice, or bodice to skirt.

JUMPER

Sleeveless, one-piece garment with low-cut neckline and room under armhole to allow for blouse, sweater, etc. May be street length or floor length, depending on fashion trend.

JUMPSUIT

A garment of pants and bodice joined as one.

JUNIOR

See FIGURE TYPE. Pattern selection for the well proportioned, shorter back waist length figure, about 5'4" tall.

JUNIOR PETITE

See FIGURE TYPE. Pattern selection for the well-developed petite figure with fullest hip measurement 7" below waist. Height approximately 5' to 5'1".

JUTE

A fiber from an East Indian plant used chiefly in burlap, sacking, and some twines.

K

KAPOK

A filling for seat cushions, pillows, mattresses, and soft toys, etc.

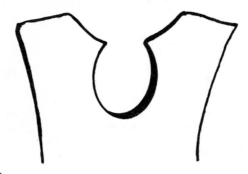

KEYHOLE

A round neckline with rounded or wedge-shaped opening at front.

KICK PLEAT

See PLEAT. Pleat on narrow skirt at lower edge, needed for ease when walking or bending; may be box, knife, or an inverted pleat.

KILT

See PLEAT. A short, knife-pleated, wrap-around skirt, associated with Scottish origin, which traditionally closes at the waist with a buckle and is held closed over the thigh with a kilt pin.

KILT PIN

A style of safety pin, usually about 3″ or more long, used to close a kilt over the thigh.

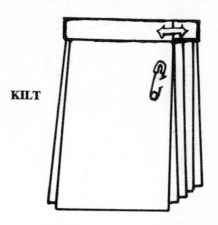

KILT

KIMONO

A robe with loose, wide sleeves, fastened at waist with an obi (Japanese sash); also sleeve description.

KIMONO SLEEVE

Bodice of garment and sleeve cut in one piece. May or may not have seam or dart at shoulder. Bottom of sleeve is loose and wide.

KNIFE PLEAT

See PLEAT. Pressed folds in fabric that turn to one side of garment, equal in width and pressed down to hem.

KNIT FABRIC

Fabric composed of a series of tiny loops of one or more yarns which "give" and then reshape themselves without strain. Made up of many fibers such as wool, polyester or cotton. There are single- and double-knits; single-knits are lightweight and soft, excellent for soft folds and draping, also for T-shirts and lounge-wear. Double-knits are usually firm and stable—generally for suits and pants. When using knit fabrics, use "with nap" layout of pattern, since fabric is constructed on looms in one direction and there may be slight differences in light reflection. Be sure stretch of fabric is "around" the body when cutting. Use ballpoint or "all-in-one" needle when stitching to prevent snags and skipped stitches; throat plate with small hole reduces puckering.

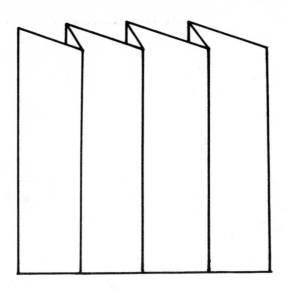

KNIFE PLEAT

KNIT SEAM

A seam made on knit fabrics by using a medium stitch length and stretching fabric as seam is being stitched. Stretching the fabric prevents broken stitches. It is not necessary to stretch knit fabric when using a small zigzag or built-in stretch stitch.

KNITTING

The making of fabric by using two or more pointed needles to knot strands of yarns together by forming connecting loops.

KNOT STITCH

A securing stitch at beginning and end of stitching. Also called lockstitch.

L

LACE

Fine, open-work fabric made into designs formed by knotted, twisted threads on a net background. Used as a trim or for entire garment.

LAME

Fabric woven with metallic threads, sometimes combined with other fibers in plain or fancy weaves. Used mainly for evening wear.

LAMBSWOOL

Soft, fleecy fabric used in padding and underlinings. Excellent quality.

LAMINATED FABRIC

Two fabrics joined by foam or adhesives to form one fabric.

LAP

Any edge placed over another, as on a continuous placket on shirt cuffs.

LAP BOARD

A board with a flat surface and contoured inner edge, placed near the body when sitting to do hand sewing in a chair, rather than at a table. It rests on the arms of a chair for support or sometimes has legs.

LAPEL

Upper part of garment, between top button and collar, that turns back. Seen on coats, suits, and coat-like dresses.

LAPPED SEAM

One seam allowance is folded under and placed over other seam allowance, then topstitched; used on yokes and gussets.

LAPPED ZIPPER

A fastening using conventional neckline zipper, with fabric extended over, and concealing one side of inserted zipper. Used on lightweight garments and sportswear. Heavier zippers are available for slipcovers and home-decorating projects.

LAWN

Sheer, thin crisp-finished cotton.

LAYERING

See BEVELING.

LAYOUT

See PATTERN LAYOUT.

LAZY DAISY STITCH

Embroidery stitch that resembles a chain stitch, used to form a flower.

LEATHERETTE

Imitation leather.

LENGTHWISE GRAIN

Yarns in fabric that run in the same direction as selvage. It is stronger and has less "give" or stretch than crosswise grain.

LETTUCE EDGE

The ruffled edge on knit garments formed by stretching fabric while zigzag stitching close to garment edge; when stretch is released, the edge forms a curly ruffle resembling edge of leaf lettuce.

LINE

The effect a style gives by the construction and design of a garment.

LINEN

A fabric outstanding in strength made from natural flax fibers. Usually in a plain, lustrous weave. It comes in several weights: sheer, for handkerchiefs, and fine garments; dressweight and heavier, for tailored clothes. Often used in the making of tablecloths.

LINGERIE

Women's undergarments that are lightweight, such as slips, bras, panties.

LINGERIE HEM

A hand-rolled hem made with overcast stitches evenly spaced, forming puffs or small scallops.

LINGERIE SEAM

Sturdy seams stitched together, pressed to one side and zigzag stitched through all layers along seam edge.

LINING

Lightweight fabric inside a finished garment concealing construction of seams, etc. Makes garment look nicer and become more durable; prevents garment from stretching, and helps retain its shape. Draperies are lined to prevent fading; lining gives added body and protects fabric. Bedspreads may also be lined.

LINK BUTTONS

Two buttons held together with thread or chain; used as cuff links.

LOCKSTITCH

Overlap stitch used to secure thread at beginning and end of seam by machine; also called backstitch.

LOOM

Machine or frame used in weaving cloth.

LOOP

A fastening which extends beyond finished edge of garment held together by a button. Used on dresses, jackets, coats, etc. May be of purchased corded tubing. Sometimes, at back neck opening, a loop is formed with thread, using the hand chain stitch.

LOOP TURNER

A specially designed tool with a latch-hook device on one end and a rounded circle for the finger on the other. It is used for turning cording and tubing to right side. May be used for pulling elastic through casings.

LUSTER

The shine or sheen of fiber or fabric.

M

MACHINE BASTING

The longest stitch on machine, used in place of hand-basting. When temporarily stitched for garment fitting, stitches should be exactly on seamline. They can be removed easily by cutting threads of upper layer every few stitches and pulling out the lower thread.

MACHINE BUTTONHOLE

Opening on garment for button to pass through, made after garment is completed. Done by machine with thread passing through main fabric, the interfacing, and the facing; worked with a zigzag stitch.

MACHINE HEM

A hem that is completely finished by machine. Found on sportswear and home decorating items, such as bedspreads, slipcovers, etc.

MACHINE STITCH

See STITCHES. The stitching of seams or finished edges by machine. When stitching seams permanently, beginning and end of seam are usually reinforced with a machine backstitch.

MACRAME

Cord-like knotted lace worked into many patterns. Done by hand or woven on looms. It is used for belts, hangings for plants or walls, for trim, and many other projects.

MADRAS

Woven cotton fabric usually in brightly colored plaids. Characteristic of fabric is the "bleeding" of colors when fabric is laundered. Separate hand or machine washing is recommended.

MAGNET

A handy gadget that will pick up pins and needles that have fallen. Many shears have magnetic blades.

MALINE

Hexagon-shaped net or mesh used for veiling and millinery.

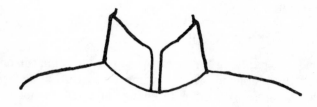

MANDARIN

See COLLAR. Collar style with curved or straight edge. Stands straight up.

MAN-MADE FIBERS

Filaments or fibers that do not have natural fibrous forms, such as chemically produced synthetics, and mineral substances such as glass.

MARGIN

Excess tissue outside cutting line on pattern piece. Margin will fall away when cutting through pattern and fabric on cutting line. These margins are handy to use when making pattern adjustments.

MARKING

Any method used to transfer construction symbols from pattern to fabric.

MARKING GAUGE

See SEWING GAUGE.

MATCHING

Joining together markings, notches and all fabrics so that they should align together accurately.

MATERNITY

See FIGURE TYPE. Pattern selection with extra ease for the pregnant woman. The usual sizes should be purchased, since pattern is designed to include maternity ease as needed.

MATTE FINISH

Fabric with a dull surface.

MAXI

Skirt length which finishes between calf of leg and ankle.

MEASUREMENT GUIDE

Body measurements taken for pattern selection and for adjusting pattern for perfect fit, allowing for design and ease:

BACK WIDTH	HIP
BACK WAIST LENGTH	NECK
BUST	SHOULDER LENGTH
CHEST	SHOULDER TO BUST
CROTCH	WAIST
FRONT WAIST LENGTH	WAIST TO FLOOR

MELTON CLOTH

Firmly woven woolen fabric used for undercollar on men's jackets, giving shape and durability to collar; also for coats and outer garments.

MEN

See FIGURE TYPE. Pattern selection. Select according to neck size; chest, waist, and sleeve length may be adjusted. Shorts and slacks should be according to waist measurement; crotch, hip, and length may be adjusted.

MENDING TAPE

Adhesive tape used in areas that need extra reinforcement. The heat of iron will bond tape to fabric, eliminating stitching.

MERCERIZED

Special finish adding strength and luster to cotton fabric.

METRIC MEASUREMENTS

The measurements of the body, yardage or any notion, sewing equipment, and all items that are needed for constructing a garment. See back of book for metric conversion chart for changes from inches and yardage to millimeters, centimeters and meters.

MIDDY

Blouse with a sailor collar; slips over the head.

MIDI

Hem finished at mid-calf.

MILAN LACE

Tape or braid in floral or scroll design on a net background.

MILIUM

Treated lining fabric, with metal insulation giving warmth in winter, coolness in summer.

MINI

Short hemlength, ending at thigh.

MISS

See FIGURE TYPE. Pattern selection. Considered the average figure type. Height 5′5″ tall with average waist length and bust position.

MISS PETITE

See FIGURE TYPE. Pattern selection for the shorter, well-proportioned figure, height 5′2″ to 5′3″ without shoes.

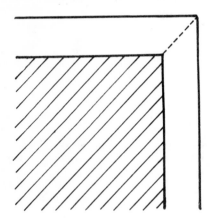

MITER

The diagonal seam formed when fabric is joined at a square corner of a hem or straight band. Reduces bulk and enables corner to lie smooth.

MOCK TURTLENECK COLLAR

Type of neckline which has stand-up collar; usually has zipper closing at back of garment.

MODE

Fashion, or style.

MOHAIR

See ANGORA.

MOIRE

A wavy finish on corded or ribbed fabrics of silk, cotton, and blends. Most moiré is taffeta.

MONOGRAM

Closely-worked flat stitches placed against each other forming initials or letters of the alphabet.

MONOGRAMMER

See SEWING MACHINE ACCESSORY. Special sewing machine accessory which enables the sewer to produce professionally finished monograms. May be purchased in several sizes from A to Z. Ideal on hand towels, sheets, blouses, ties, etc.

MOTIF

Design, decoration.

MOUNTING

See UNDERLINING. Two layers of fabric sewn together as one.

MUSLIN

Cotton fabric used for making duplicate of garments for correct fitting and design. These muslins become an exact pattern for use with more expensive fabrics. Frequently used for quilting and home decorating.

N

NAP

Short fibers on surface of fabric that lie in one direction when brushed, e.g., velvet, fake fur. When laying out pattern for cutting, each piece must be placed on fabric with all pieces in one direction, following "with nap" layout.

NAP LAYOUT

See WITH NAP.

NATURAL

Unbleached or undyed fabric or yarn.

NATURAL FIBERS

Fibers from animals, vegetables, or minerals that are made into fabric or yarns, i.e., wool taken from sheep, cotton from plants, silk from silk worms, linen from flax plants and metallics from minerals.

NECK

Body measurement taken around neck, just above collar bone.

NECKBAND, or STAND

Neckline with collar that turns down over an added piece of fabric. Seen on hand-tailored shirts. The neckband usually has a button closing.

NEEDLE

A strong, metal sewing tool with point at one end and a hole for thread at the other, used for hand or machine sewing. Machine needles differ from hand needles. When purchasing needles for hand sewing, remember that the higher the number, the finer the fabric to be sewn. *Sharps* have small, round eyes, used for general sewing, are medium length. *Betweens* are shorter length for fine work. *Embroidery or crewel* are used for decorative sewing and have a longer eye for heavier threads. *Cotton darners* are similar to embroidery or crewel, but longer to make weaving of threads easier. *Leather needle* is three-corner-pointed for sewing leather and fur. *Machine needles*: the higher the size number, the heavier the fabric to be used. Average size is #14. Special needles can be purchased for sewing leather. If skipped stitches appear on fabric when sewing, needle may be blunt or bent, inserted backward, threaded incorrectly, or the wrong size. Special ball-point needles are recommended when this happens; they may also be used for knit fabrics to prevent pulls in fabric.

NEEDLE BOARD

A device used for pressing velvet, velveteen and other high-pile fabrics. It is made with a bed of needles angled carefully so that the pile of the fabric falls between them to prevent matting; to be used with steam or dry iron.

NEEDLEPOINT

Hand embroidery creating designs on mesh canvas, by working yarn through fabric.

NEEDLE THREADER

A small device that has a wire attachment to simplify threading a needle.

NEEDLEWORK

All work done with a needle and thread, including sewing, embroidery, crocheting, or knitting.

NET

Sheer, open-work fabric with knots at square corners, ranging from fine tulle to coarse fishnet.

NON-WOVEN FABRIC

Fabric which is neither spun, knitted nor woven. It consists of mats of fibers held together by bonding agents or which interlock, e.g., Pellon.

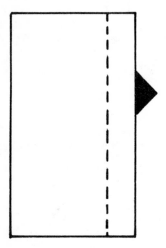

NOTCH

Small, diamond-shaped cutout on cutting edge of pattern, indicating which edges are to be joined together when stitching seams. Generally, they are numbered, which facilitates placing pattern for matching plaids and stripes.

NOTCHED COLLAR

Type of neckline which has a rolled collar with lapels added. Collar always has a lapped-over front opening, e.g., blazer jacket. *See also* COLLAR.

NOTIONS

The buttons, zippers, seam binding, thread, etc., needed to complete a garment during construction.

NYLON

Strong, resilient man-made fiber or yarn. Blends well with other fibers. Washes easily, dries quickly, and needs little or no ironing.

NYLON CLOSURE TAPE

A two-part fastening tape which simply presses closed and pulls open, eliminating the need for buttons, etc. One part of tape is a strip covered with nylon hooks which cling to the other part of the tape, which is pile-covered. Allows trims to be easily removed and makes closures adjustable. Excellent for children's wear, waistbands, etc.

O

OBI

Wide sash of Japanese origin, used at waistline.

OMBRE

A fabric dyeing process that produces colors or shades of one color varying from lighter to darker.

ONE-WAY DESIGN

Fabrics that have distinct designs facing one direction. When using these fabrics follow "with nap" layout for cutting. All pattern pieces must be laid on fabric with design and pattern facing one way.

ONE-WAY STRETCH

Fabric reference. The stretch of a knit fabric in one direction. When working with knit fabrics, the "stretch" should be horizontal on the body for proper fit.

ON GRAIN

The perfect right angle of lengthwise and crosswise threads of fabric. *See* GRAIN.

OPEN WORK

Insertions of decorative open designs, hand- or machine-made.

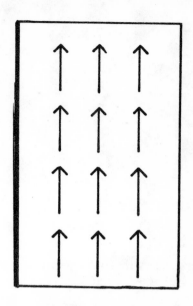

ONE-WAY DESIGN

OPTIONAL

Back of pattern envelopes use this term when referring to buttons, top stitching, bows or trim on a garment. These may or may not be used. They are simply there as a design.

ORGANDY

Thin, transparent cotton fabric, permanently stiff, with a plain weave.

ORGANZA

Fine, sheer fabric similar to organdy, made in silk and synthetic fibers.

OUTSEAM

The seam from waist to finished hem.

OUTSIDE

The right side; the finished side.

OVERBLOUSE

Blouse that is not worn inside skirt, pants, etc., but outside or over the bottom garment.

OVERCAST STITCH

Hand-stitch used to prevent raw edges from raveling by taking slanted stitches over the cut edge, evenly spaced and uniformly deep.

OVEREDGE FOOT

See SEWING MACHINE ACCESSORY. Machine foot that may be used to produce overedge stitching on seams and edges of fabric to prevent raveling of cut edges; also used decoratively on edges of place mats, shades, etc.

OVERHAND STITCH

This stitch, done by hand, holds two finished edges together. Often used in attaching lace edging or ribbon to garment. Placing right sides together take small stitches over edges about $\frac{1}{16}''$ apart and continue, over and over the edge, until completed.

OVERLAP

Any part of a garment that extends over another, as in the opening of a coat, or at the extended edge of a waistband.

OVERLAY

Pattern piece used to change an original pattern. Taped or pinned into position on basic pattern, it is cut as one.

OVERSKIRT

Extra skirt worn over another skirt, gown, slacks, etc. Used decoratively and often seen in sheer fabrics.

P

PADDING

Soft, bulky wadding or materials made of cotton, wool, and blends, used to stuff or pad such items as coat linings and shoulder pads; also used in quilting.

PADDING STITCH

See STITCHES. A hand-stitch, small and diagonally shaped, used in tailoring to hold interfacings firmly to garment. These stitches are carefully sewed, as they should not appear on right side of garment.

PANNE

A finish for velvet or satin, produced by pressure, which gives velvet a satiny sheen and satin a smoother and more lustrous surface.

PANTS/TROUSERS

Garment with leg parts, beginning at waistline and ending at ankle.

PANTS SUIT

Women's two-piece outfit, consisting of jacket and pants, and sometimes a vest.

PARALLEL

A line that at all points is an equal distance from another line or selvage edge.

98

PASSEMENTERIE BRAID

Tubular-shaped braid that can be coiled and shaped into designs and stitched to fabric; can be purchased in ready-made designs as a trim.

PATCH

A small piece of fabric used in a given area to strengthen or to reinforce a corner, elbow, knee, or torn area.

PATTERN

A carefully designed blueprint, marked on tissue paper, showing construction details of a particular garment or object. Patterns may be classified in three categories: *conventional*: suitable for woven fabric and firm knits. Basic ease allowance for design and fit, is included in pattern. *Recommended for knits*: same basic ease allowance as the conventional pattern, but style and lines are especially good for knits. *Stretchable knits only*: smaller than other patterns of same size and style. Less ease is incorporated in pattern which is designed to utilize the stretch of fabric for shaping and ease. Such patterns should not be used for firm knits or woven fabrics.

PATTERN CATALOG

A large, bound book showing many different pattern illustrations from which the home sewer may select. Sections are separated by tabs according to figure types, garment, style, and speciality items. It contains numerical index pages and body measurement charts for easy reference. These catalogs are revised monthly to include latest fashions.

PATTERN ENVELOPE

Package containing pattern pieces and cutting and sewing directions. The envelope itself gives vital information on selection of fabric, yardage, and notions. Shows a sketch or photograph of completed garment and other special information needed to achieve the effect for which the designer has aimed.

PATTERN LAYOUT

The way pattern pieces are to be placed on fabric for cutting. Guide sheet shows diagrams for different widths of fabric, pattern size, and view to be used.

PATTERN PAPER

Wide paper with 1" square markings that enables a pattern to be traced on to it.

PATTERN REPEAT

Amount of space occupied by each complete design on fabric.

PATTERN SELECTION

See FIGURE TYPE.

PEAU DE SOIE

French fabric term for "skin of silk," made in soft, good quality silk, satin, or synthetics, with a dull surface.

PEIGNOIR

The robe worn over a matching nightgown.

PELLON

Non-woven fabric that does not ravel; used as interfacing.

PELT

Animal skin with fur remaining.

PEPLUM

Garment design with fullness at hip, extended from bodice to hipline.

PERCALE

Firmly-woven lightweight cotton fabric with smooth surface. Used for fine sheets and as a dress fabric.

PEPLUM

PERMANENT BASTING

Any machine-basting stitched into garment that will not later be removed.

PERPENDICULAR

Two lines meeting at a right angle.

PETER PAN

See COLLAR. Collar type that lies flat and has rounded corners.

PICK STITCH

Hand-stitch used mainly for a decorative effect. It is sewn only through top layer of fabric and resembles prick stitch.

PICK UP LINE

Fold-line on center of dart or tuck.

PICOT EDGE

Fine machine-stitch appearing as tiny scallops. Edge is finished by cutting close to stitching line.

PIECE DYED

The addition of dye to fabric after being woven or knitted.

PIECE GOODS

Fabric sold in cut lengths or by the yard.

PIECING

The stitching together of two pieces of fabric to form more width needed in a given area. Generally seen on circular skirts. This extra fabric should always be cut on grain. This method is also used in creating new fabric by joining small sections together, as in making patchwork quilts.

PILE

The raised surface of such fabrics as velvet and fake fur. The direction of pile, when positioned for sewing, affects its appearance.

PILE-WEAVE

Fabric reference. Surface of fabric is raised slightly and forms cut or looped yarns, such as terry cloth, corduroy or velvet. Weave is produced by interlacing three sets of yarn, one of which is either cut or looped.

PIPING

A bias, corded trim used for decorative seam accents. May be inserted in seams at necklines, cuffs, etc.; also used for corded buttonholes.

PIQUE

Term referring to a fabric, generally of cotton, that has raised, lengthwise cords in various widths and novelty designs, e.g., birds-eye and waffle.

PIN

Small, pointed implement. Various types of pins are available: rustproof dressmaker's pins; stainless steel silk pins (these do not leave marks in fabric when removed); ballpoint pins with or without colored heads (excellent for knit fabrics since they separate the fibers instead of piercing them, preventing pulls). Pins are used to hold patterns and fabric together, and all during garment construction.

PINAFORE

Apron-like sleeveless dress that is worn over another garment.

PIN BASTING

The pinning together of seams or darts on stitching lines before actually sewing.

PINCH PLEATS

Group of pleats used on heading of drapery. One pleat is divided into smaller pleats which are stitched together as one group of pleats.

PINCUSHION

A small, filled cushion to hold pins. Some cushions have a smaller, attached emery bag for sharpening and removing rust from pins and needles. There is also a bracelet-type pincushion for convenience when sewing and fitting.

PIN-FITTING

The pinning of garment pieces together for fitting before permanently stitching.

PINK

To finish an edge, by cutting with pinking shears, of seams, facings, etc.; this helps to reduce raveling.

PINKING SHEARS

See SCISSORS.

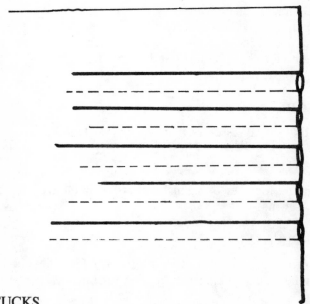

PIN-TUCKS

Tucks that are pressed and stitched on the very edge of fold.

PINWALE

Raised ribs found in fabrics such as corduroy.

PIVOT

To turn a corner in machine stitching by leaving needle in fabric, lifting the presser foot, and turning the material in a different direction.

PLACEMENT LINE

Line on pattern indicating where pockets, buttonholes, pleats, etc., are to be placed during garment construction.

PLACKET

Visible strip of fabric overlapping an opening in garment; finished with zipper, snaps, or other closures allowing for ease in dressing.

PLAID

A design of fabric in which colored stripes or bars cross each other at right angles. Also known as tartan, of Scottish origin.

PLAIN SEAM

See SEAM. Two pieces of fabric stitched with right sides together, ⅝" from cut edge; sometimes called regular seam.

PLAIN WEAVE

A simple, fundamental type of weave in which filling yarns are passed over and under each warp yarn.

PLEAT

A fold of fabric in a given area which may be stitched down, pressed, partially stitched, or left loose. On pattern pieces pleats are indicated by alternating solid and broken lines; an arrow shows direction of pleating. Used as decoration or in controlling fullness of garment.

PLISSE

Cotton fabric with a puckered effect. Made in a variety of fabrics of many weights, e.g., lawn, organdy.

PLUNGING

Style of neckline that is cut lower than usual, revealing breast curves.

POCKETING FABRIC

Durable, twill-woven cotton fabric with a soft, shiny surface. Comes in various weights. May also be used for reinforcing areas of potential strain.

POINT PRESSER

Pressing aid, made of wood, with many points and curves. Used for pressing open the seams in points of collars and lapels and used generally in tailoring.

POINT TURNER AND CREASER

A flat tool with both a pointed end and a rounded end. The pointed end is used to push out points in collars, corners on jackets, pockets, etc.; the rounded end is used when ironing to flatten seams.

POLYESTER

Man-made fibers formed into fabric, thread or yarn. 100 percent polyester is completely washable, never needs ironing, and will retain its shape. Comes in blends with wool, cotton, etc. The higher percentage of polyester, the more wrinkle-resistant the fabric will be.

POUNDING BLOCK, or CLAPPER

A block of wood used to flatten seams after they have been steam-pressed open. The block is slapped down on the seam and held for a second or two. Especially good for enclosed seams, tailored clothes, and hard-to-press wools; sometimes called a beater.

PRE-FOLD

The folding of garment sections or binding and pressing before applying to a given area. Some bindings are sold pre-folded.

PRE-SHAPE

Shaping, by steaming with iron, pieces of fabric that are curved and are to fit into a similar area.

PRE-SHRINK

Treatment of fabric before cutting, by laundering or dry cleaning, so that its dimensions do not change. Many fabrics are pre-shrunk by the manufacturer.

PRESSER FOOT

See SEWING MACHINE ACCESSORY. The part of the sewing machine that holds fabric steady while stitching. Various types are available.

PRESSING

The press and lift motion used with an iron that applies heat and moisture firmly to an area. It is important to avoid stretching when pressing knit fabrics.

PRESSING CLOTHS

Specific materials laid over garments when ironing. Excellent in preventing shine, scorch, and lint. Made in several types of fiber: wool—to be used on wool fabrics; canvas—to be used on heavier weight fabrics; muslin, or cheesecloth—to be used on lightweight fabrics; see-through cloths—convenient on all fabrics.

PRESSING MITT

A padded cushion which fits over the hand while ironing small, hard-to-reach areas. Allows movement of hand inside cushion to reach inside sleeves, sleeve-caps, pockets, etc.

PRESSURE

The amount of force of the sewing machine's presser foot. Fabric should feed through machine easily, without strain or slack. When pressure is too great, upper layer of fabric will bubble. Adjustment of pressure should be greater for lightweight fabrics, lower for heavier fabrics.

PRICK STITCH

A style of backstitch which forms a tiny stitch on top part of garment and an overlapped stitch on the bottom. Done by hand and seen on hand-stitched zippers. Similar to hand-pick stitch, except that the prick stitch is visible on underside of garment.

PRINCESS LINE

Seams of a garment style that are shaped and contoured to body curves.

PRINTING

A process by which colors forming designs are applied to fabrics.

PROPORTION

Space division of design. The balance and scale of a wardrobe in co-ordinating color, texture, and fabric. Also refers to figure types, e.g., "well proportioned" means fully developed, evenly distributed.

PUCKER

The little ripples that sometimes appear on seamlines. Reduced pressure and lower tension on the machine will control puckering.

PURITAN

See COLLAR. Flat collar similar to Peter Pan collar, but larger, extending below collar bone. Sometimes has points at collar tips, instead of curves.

Q

QUARTERING

The division into four equal parts of elastic, fabric, or trim before adding to similarly divided area.

QUILTER

See SEWING MACHINE ACCESSORY. Special foot for sewing machine that is designed for stitching lightly-padded fabrics. Excellent for following curves, shapes, and floral designs.

QUILTING

Several layers of fabric stitched together to form designs.

R

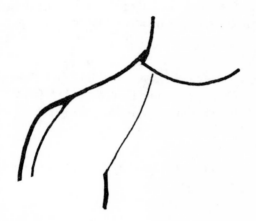

RAGLAN SLEEVE

Sleeve style which has a seam running diagonally from neck edge to underarm.

RASCHEL

Type of warp knit, coarse and of lacy openwork design, giving appearance of hand-made knit.

RAVEL

Small, loose threads that fall away from woven fabrics at cut edges. These edges should be finished off to prevent raveling, by overcasting, pinking, binding, etc. *Also:* threads pulled away from cut edges of woven fabric to form a fringe.

RAW EDGE

Edge of fabric that has not been finished.

RECOVERY POWER

The ability of stretch fabric or elastic to return to its original shape after it has been stretched.

REGULATION STITCH

See STITCHES. Machine stitch which is permanent when constructing a garment. Stitch length and tension vary according to fabric used. On most medium-weight fabrics, stitch length is generally 12 stitches to the inch. Sheer fabrics require shorter stitches; heavy fabrics and knits require longer stitches.

REINFORCE

To strengthen any area subjected to strain by adding extra stitches, underlays of fabric or strips of tape.

RELEASE DART

See DART TUCK.

REMNANT

Left-over piece of fabric.

RETURN

Extra fabric on curtains or draperies required from the curve of rod to the wall. The distance from this end to wall is the "return."

REVERS

Lapels on garments of coats and suits that are wide and shaped.

REVERSIBLE FABRIC

Fabric that is finished on both sides. Either side may be used face-out. *See* DOUBLE-FACED.

111

REWEAVE

A method of repairing a hole in fabric by weaving threads taken from an unseen area of garment, such as facing or hems. Strands of thread are woven across the area of the hole, retaining the design of fabric.

RIB

A straight, raised cord on fabrics, running lengthwise, crosswise, or diagonally in woven fabric.

RIBBON

Narrow, woven strips of fabric, such as satin, velvet, silk, or grosgrain, finished at both edges; used as a trim.

RIB KNIT

Very stretchable fabric with a pattern of raised ribs or of knit and purl stitches, as in a sweater.

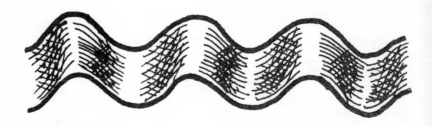

RICKRACK

Zigzag shaped, decorative edging for border or top-trim for fashion apparel, craft items, and home decorating; it goes easily around curves.

RIGHT SIDE

The top side of fabric; the finished side; the outside of garment.

RIP

To remove unwanted stitches; tearing fabric to straighten grain.

RISE

The distance from crotch to waist area on pant-type garments.

ROBE

Coat-like garment worn over sleepwear.

ROLL

To conceal seams by manipulating fabric between fingers on curve and fold of a collar or on similar fold on pocket flaps. Pad-stitching or pressing helps shape this area and keep the seams out of sight.

ROLLER FOOT

See SEWING MACHINE ACCESSORY. Specially designed foot for sewing machine, enabling the sewer to easily stitch fabrics requiring special handling, such as velvet, leather, or matching designs. Little wheels under the foot roll over fabric when stitching, thereby keeping top layer and bottom layer even.

ROLLER PRINTING

See DIRECT PRINTING.

ROLL LINE

Marking sometimes found on a pattern indicating area along which the collar and lapel are turned back.

RUFFLE

A band of fabric that is gathered or pleated then added to an edge for decoration or additional length.

RUFFLER

See SEWING MACHINE ACCESSORY. A machine accessory offering the sewer a simple and quick method of gathering and pleating ruffles evenly. May be adjusted to several different widths. Ruffles may be formed and attached in one operation. See machine manual for instructions.

RULER

A flat, straight-edged tool with numbers for measuring and ruling lines for placement of buttons, pleats, etc.; lengths vary. A plastic see-through type retains its straight edge and will not warp.

RUNNING STITCH

Simple, hand-stitch, used for quilting, mending, tucking, gathering. Should be no more than ¼" long. Pass threaded needle through fabric several times, using an in-and-out motion, then pull needle through.

RUN-OF-THE-MILL

Fabrics often below standard, sometimes referred to as "seconds."

S

SADDLE STITCH

Decorative hand-stitch used for distinct topstitching. Stitches are placed ¼″ apart, using buttonhole twist thread or embroidery floss.

SAFETY PIN

Rounded pin that is held closed by means of a safety catch on one side, holding point of pin securely in place.

SAG

The stretch or droop that occurs on bias-cut garments when hung incorrectly. The stretching of an area of a garment that will not return to its original shape.

SAILCLOTH

A very heavy, strong, plain weave fabric. Made of cotton, linen, or jute. Excellent for outdoor furniture.

SAILOR COLLAR

A collar extended from a "V" line at neck front to a square at the back. Sometimes called "middy."

SANFORIZED

A trademark, meaning fabric that will not shrink more than 1 percent in washing.

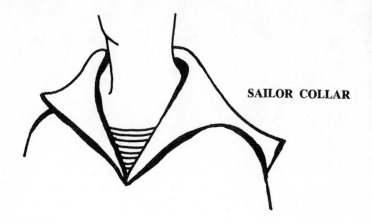

SAILOR COLLAR

SASH

Scarf or band worn around the waist.

SATEEN

Cotton cloth with a highly lustrous satin weave; used as lining.

SATIN

Fabric of very slippery silk or man-made fibers, the surface of which is highly lustrous. Used for evening wear, linings and home decorating.

SATIN STITCH

A hand or machine embroidery stitch. Closely worked, flat stitches placed against each other, forming designs or initials.

SCALLOP

A semi-circular edge finish.

SCISSORS

A cutting tool, necessary for accuracy in cutting fabric and trim and finishing seams and other areas during garment construction. There are several types and sizes: 1. *Bent handle shears*: blades measuring 7″ or more in length with one small opening for thumb and a larger opening for two or more fingers. Best for control and balance when cutting fabric. Left- and right-hand shears are available. 2. *Trimming scissors*: ranging in size from 3½″ or more with two rounded openings for fingers; used for delicate cutting and trimming. 3. *Pinking or scalloping shears*: special shears with zigzag or scalloped blades; used on fabrics that fray easily. 4. *Electric scissors*: for fast cutting; can be battery operated or plugged directly into current. 5. *Thread clips*: short, equal blades with spring mechanism to keep blades apart; used for clipping stray threads quickly. 6. *Buttonhole scissors*: small scissors with an adjustable screw, making it possible to cut open different buttonhole lengths.

SCREEN PRINTING

A process of applying colored design onto fabric, using a silk, nylon, or metal screen.

SEAM

The joined line of two or more pieces of fabric, or the stitching line of a fold in a single fabric piece, as in a dart.

SEAM ALLOWANCE

Fabric between seamline and cut edge. This width is normally ⅝″ on all patterns, unless otherwise indicated on pattern pieces.

SEAM BINDING

Ribbon, lace, or binding that is sewn over fabric and hems to conceal raw edge.

SEAM EDGE

The cut edge of seam allowance.

SEAM FINISH

Any method of finishing a raw edge to prevent raveling: binding, pinking, stitching.

SEAM GUIDE

See SEWING MACHINE ACCESSORY. A magnetic or screw-on type of machine accessory which helps sew perfect seams. Set guide to desired distance from needle; stitch with cut edge of fabric against raised, flat edge of guide.

SEAMLINE

Stitching line on pattern piece, indicated by broken lines usually ⅝" from cutting edge. Width of seam may vary in certain areas.

SEAM RIPPER, or STITCH RIPPER

Pen-shaped tool with pointed end and curved, sharp edge; useful for removing unwanted stitches.

SEAM ROLL

A padded cushion used in pressing to prevent marks on outside of garment when sleeve seams are pressed open.

SEAM TAPE, or SEAM LACE

Flat, ribbon-like fabric or lace with a woven, finished edge, usually ½"-¾" wide; used to finish hem edges or as a reinforcement.

SECURE

To fasten permanently, using a knot or backstitching, etc.

SEERSUCKER

Fabric of lightweight cotton blend with crinkled stripes running lengthwise on fabric. Made by setting some warp yarns tight and others loose.

SELF

A sewing term for "same," as in the use of the same material for both the trim and the garment itself.

SELF-BOUND SEAM

An enclosed seam. After making plain seam, trim one seam allowance to ¼", then fold under other seam allowance down to seam line and hand or machine stitch, enclosing the seam.

SELVAGE

The finished, lengthwise edge of woven fabrics.

SEMI-FITTED

Not fitted too closely to natural figure lines.

SEPARATING ZIPPER

Zipper with openings at both ends, designed for use on sweaters and jackets that must open completely down front. Comes in light- and heavyweight and in many lengths.

SET-IN-LINING

Lining that is fully attached including at the bottom edge of garment.

SEWING GAUGE/KNITTING GAUGE

6" ruler with moveable indicator, convenient for measuring short distances.

SEWING MACHINE

A carefully constructed mechanical tool used for sewing. Machines can straight-stitch, zigzag, make buttonholes, sew on buttons, sew a blind hem, and make many decorative stitches. There are many styles, designed to fit everyone's needs and skills.

SEWING MACHINE ACCESSORY

Separate machine part that may be supplied with sewing machine or purchased individually to enable the sewer to achieve an accurate finish quickly. Specific parts are sold for different machines. Refer alphabetically for each accessory:

BINDER	INVISIBLE ZIPPER FOOT
BOBBIN	MONOGRAMMER
BUTTON FOOT	OVEREDGE FOOT
BUTTONHOLE FOOT	PRESSER FOOT
BUTTONHOLER	QUILTER
CAM or FASHION DISC	ROLLER FOOT
CHAIN STITCH	RUFFLER
EDGE STITCHER	SEAM GUIDE
EVEN FEED FOOT	SPECIAL PURPOSE FOOT
FINGER GUARD	SPOOL PIN
GATHERING FOOT	STRAIGHT STITCH FOOT
GENERAL PURPOSE FOOT	TUCKER
HEMMER	ZIPPER FOOT

SHANK

Short, extended threads between a button and fabric. Some purchased buttons have their own shanks under button, made of plastic or metal. These threads, or stems, will allow sufficient room for garment buttonhole to fit smoothly over button.

SHAPING MATERIALS

Fabrics used to give additional body to a garment, such as interfacings, linings, underlinings, or interlinings.

SHAWL

Triangular-shaped material worn around shoulders.

SHAWL COLLAR

Neckline where upper collar and lapel are cut in one piece, forming a roll on collar when turned down. Seen on many wrap-around coats, robes, and sweaters.

SHEARS

See SCISSORS.

SHEATH

Dress style; close-fitting with a straight skirt.

SHEER

Transparent fabric, e.g., chiffon, organza.

SHELL EDGE

A hand-sewn, narrow hem that is done by taking small stitches over the edge at measured intervals, forming small scallops; seen on lingerie.

121

SHIFT

A loose-fitting dress.

SHIRRING

Two or more rows of gathering, used decoratively to control full-ness in fabric.

SHIRTWAIST

Dress with shirt-like bodice.

SHORTS

Short-legged pants or trousers usually ending above knee.

SHOULDER LENGTH

Measurement taken on body from base of side of neck to shoulder bone at top of arm.

SHOULDER PADS

Triangular-shaped forms made of batting, lambswool or fleece, covered with muslin or cotton fabric. Used in shaping and building up the shoulder area in tailored garments.

SHOULDER TO BUST

Body measurement taken from shoulder to center of breast. Use this measurement as a guide when adjusting pattern at bust darts.

SHRINK

To contract fabric through moisture or steam, eliminating excess ease in required areas.

SILESIA

See POCKETING FABRIC. Soft, woven pocketing material of all-cotton twill; used in fine-tailored garments.

SILHOUETTE

The outline of figure; the contour of garment.

SIMPLIFIED TAILOR TACKS

See BASTE STITCH.

SINGLE-BREASTED

Center front closing with enough of an overlap on garment to allow for one row of buttons.

SIZING

A process in which a coating is applied to fabric to give it stiffness and strength. Surface of fabric is then smooth and shiny.

SKEIN

Length of yarn or thread loosely twisted and packed for use in hand knitting and crocheting.

SKIPPED STITCHES

Refers to machine stitching when stitches are not uniform in size. This sometimes happens unintentionally on synthetic fabrics that have not been pre-shrunk or when the needle size is incorrect. By using a special "all-in-one" needle or ballpoint needle this can be corrected.

SKIRT

That portion of garment below waist of dress.

SKIRT MARKER

See CHALK MARKER.

SKIVING

Technique of shaving leather on seam edges to eliminate bulk by using a skiving tool or bevel.

SLASH

A cut into fabric along a straight line. A slash is usually finished with a seam or facing.

SLASH AND SPREAD

A method of adjusting a pattern to give added width or length.

SLEEVE BOARD

Small ironing board; helpful in pressing small, hard-to-reach areas, such as sleeve seams, infant clothes, it should be well-padded.

SLEEVE CUSHION

Long, flat sleeve-shaped pad that is inserted into completed sleeve when pressing to prevent unwanted creases and wrinkles.

SLEEVE HEADS

Narrow strips placed inside the tops of sleeves to give a smooth line and support to the roll of the sleeve cap. Generally made of cotton wadding or lambswool fleece.

SLIDE FASTENER

See ZIPPER. A closure with little teeth or coils and a pull tab to open or close a garment.

SLIDE PLATE

Movable metal part on sewing machine that slides open to allow access to bobbin.

SLIP BASTING

A temporary hand-stitch used when matching plaids and designs before permanently stitching them together. Stitching is done from right side of fabric.

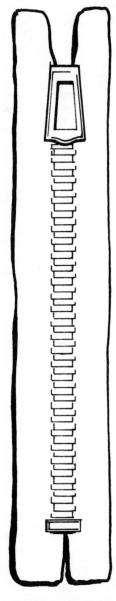

SLIDE FASTENER

125

SLIP STITCH

Tiny invisible hand-stitch taken through fold of fabric, used when attaching pockets, tie ends of waistbands, and linings into jackets or coats.

SLIT

Lengthwise cut; also long, narrow opening.

SLOPER

Individual or custom-fitted templates of a basic pattern, used as a pattern base from which various styles can be made. Shows dart points, notches, grain line arrows, but no seam allowances or hemlines.

SLOT SEAM

A decorative seam used mostly on tailored garments, made by sewing an underlay of fabric under a basted seam, then removing basted stitches.

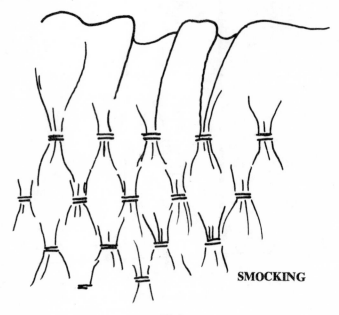

SMOCKING

SMOCKING

Hand-embroidery stitches used to control fullness, by forming decorative gathers.

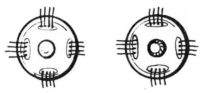

SNAP FASTENER

A metal, two-part, flat closure with one part having a cup-shaped section and the other a small protruding knob. Each part is stitched separately to garment area, then pressed into each other, ensuring a neat, secure closure. Snaps may be fabric-covered for a more custom finish.

SOFT FINISH

The soft, fuzzy nap of a woolen or flannel fabric.

SOLID LINES

Markings on pattern pieces indicating center fold lines, hemlines, pocket placement or trim. These markings should be transferred to fabric with contrasting color thread, as a guide to construction of article being sewn.

SOLUTION DYEING

The technique of dyeing synthetics while in a liquid state, imparting uniform color before being spun into fibers for producing fabrics and threads.

SOUTACHE

Narrow braid used as a trim.

SPANDEX

A man-made fabric of synthetic fibers with excellent elastic qualities; used for swimwear, undergarments, and hosiery.

SPANKING

The pounding or flattening of fabric with heat and steam to shape it. Technique used in tailoring on wool garments.

SPECIAL PURPOSE FOOT

See SEWING MACHINE ACCESSORY. Specially designed foot used for producing all kinds of decorative zigzag stitching. A raised center under foot allows closely spaced zigzag stitching to feed freely while sewing. Toes of foot hold fabric firmly. Exceptionally useful in stitching appliqués.

SPONGE

Soft wad of fibers that retains water. Excellent for dampening press cloths or fabric when extra moisture is needed to flatten seams and other areas when pressing.

SPOOL PIN

See SEWING MACHINE ACCESSORY. Short, pencil-shaped thread holder on sewing machine. Some machines have more than one spool pin enabling the sewer to do twin-needle decorative stitching used two spools of thread at the same time.

SPORTSWEAR

Casual clothing; informal wear.

STABILIZED KNIT

Knit fabric with very little stretch power.

STABILIZED SEAM

A seam that is reinforced in areas of stress by adding seam tape to strengthen and secure stitches. Seen at waistlines of knit garments and on shoulder seams.

STAY

A strip of fabric, tape, or interfacing sewn to underside of garment section to reinforce an area, holding it securely; used at waistlines, under pocket openings, at gathered areas, etc.

STAY-STITCH

A line of machine stitching placed close to seam allowance through single layer of fabric; used as a reinforcement stitch to prevent area from stretching. Placed at shoulders, curved areas and also used as a guide when folding back raw edges.

STAY TAPE

See TWILL TAPE.

STIFFENING

Term used to describe interfacings that stiffen a garment, e.g., crinoline.

STILETTO, or AWL

Sharp implement for punching holes for belt eyelets. Makes clean, sharp holes in fabrics, leather, and plastic.

STITCHES

Threads that are interlocked by hand or machine on materials to join sections together or used decoratively.

STITCH-IN-DITCH

A sewing technique used to make a finished edge, by joining self-trim and garment together with a regular seam, then folding trim over seam allowance to wrong side, and stitching in seam groove from right side, catching trim in place. Generally used on stretch fabrics, or when using bias-cut trim.

STITCHING

A term generally used in reference to any sewing.

STITCHING LINE

See SEAMLINE.

STITCH LENGTH

In machine stitching, the stitch length is determined by the number of stitches per inch: *6–8* for gathering, basting, and top stitching; *8–10* for easing and sewing with knit fabrics; *12–15* for normal sewing and curves; *15–20* for bound buttonholes and reinforcing; *finest* generally for decorative stitching.

STITCH WIDTH

Any stitch wider than straight stitch. A variety of decorative stitches can be made on sewing machines simply by changing the width of stitches, such as zigzag.

"STITCH WITCHERY"®

Fusible material placed between two layers of fabric, appliqués, or trim. When using the heat of an iron, pressing these together will fuse them to each other. Excellent for turning quick hems and many craft projects.

STOLE

Long, wide scarf to be worn around shoulders.

STRAIGHTENING FABRIC

The method of handling fabric to correct the grain line on woven fabric: selvage is snipped and a crosswise thread is pulled; then cut along the line left by the pulled thread.

STRAIGHT OF GRAIN

See GRAIN.

STRAIGHT STITCH FOOT

See SEWING MACHINE ACCESSORY. Presser foot on sewing machine having two extended toes, each a different length. Excellent for stitching on fabrics that need close control, such as fine stretch-able knits and sheers. Prevents skipped stitches on seams. Use with straight stitch throat plate.

STRAWBERRY

See EMERY CUSHION.

STRETCH KNIT FABRIC

Knitted fabric that has stretch qualities due to its construction and the use of stretch yarns; may be of polyester, wool, cotton, etc.

STRETCH SEAM BINDING

Stretchable lace edging used as an elegant finish for hems, seams and facings, especially suited for hems on knit and stretch garments.

STRETCH STITCH

Machine stitching where a backstitch is created by using a special position on machine. It is a strong, reinforcing stitch, for use on crotch areas of pants, and generally on stretch knit garments.

STRIKER

See CLAPPER.

SUEDE CLOTH

Fabric of cotton, man-made fibers, wool, or blends, knitted or woven to resemble genuine suede.

SWATCH

Small sample piece cut from fabric or trim. Used as a color guide for matching wearing apparel or purchasing zippers and other notions.

SYNTHETIC FIBERS

Man-made fibers that are chemically produced, such as acrylic, nylon, and polyester; used in the making of fabrics and threads.

T

TACK

Several stitches, taken in the same place, to hold two pieces of fabric together permanently.

TAFFETA

Crisp, lustrous, closely woven, smooth fabric with a plain weave.

TAILORING

Construction technique requiring special handling, sewing, and pressing of classic suits, coats, dresses, etc.

TAILOR'S TACKS

Small thread markings that are used as guides for pocket location, buttonholes, etc.

TAILOR'S BOARD

See POINT PRESSER.

TAILOR'S CHALK

A firm chalk made in colored squares used for marking pattern lines and fitting marks. Also available in pencil form.

TAILOR'S HAM

An oblong, firmly stuffed cushion with rounded edges. It is designed to press curved areas such as darts, princess seams, sleeve caps, or any area that requires a curved shape pressed into it; essential for tailoring. Hams should be covered in wool on one side, cotton on the other.

TAILOR'S THIMBLE

A special sewing tool sized to fit down to first joint of the finger. Open at top to expose tip of finger; used for sewing on heavy fabric. *See* THIMBLE.

TAKE-UP LEVER

The lever on a sewing machine that raises and lowers the foot.

TANK TOP

Bodice with "U"-shaped neckline in both front and back of garment.

TAPE MEASURE

A reliable flexible device needed for taking body measurements. It should be 60″ long and made of material that does not stretch or shrink. The ends should be firmly finished. It should have ⅛″ markings and be reversible. Some are made with centimeters on one side and inches on the other. The width of most tape measures is ⅝″—the same as seam allowances.

TAPER

To make smaller by cutting or stitching on a slight diagonal.

TEEN BOYS

See FIGURE TYPE. Pattern selection for taller boys who are well-proportioned but have not yet reached men's measurements. For pants, select pattern by hip size; for shirts and jackets, by neck or chest size.

TENSION

1. The parts on a sewing machine which control the correct tightness of stitches that interlock the threads of the needle and

the bobbin when stitching. 2. The degree of pull on fabric or thread.

TENT

Dress design that flows into soft folds tapering from above bust-line to hem edge.

TERRY CLOTH

A woven or knitted fabric with uncut loops on one or both sides. It is highly absorbent, requires no ironing, and is used extensively for beachwear and towels.

TEXTURE

The roughness or smoothness on the outside surface of fabric.

THIMBLE

A small sewing tool, made of plastic or metal, shaped like the tip of the middle finger and used in hand sewing. It should fit snugly on the finger; especially needed when sewing on heavy fabric. *See* TAILOR'S THIMBLE.

THREAD

Long, twisted strands of yarn made of various fibers, for machine or hand sewing. Comes in many colors and weights. Select a shade darker than fabric color, as thread sews in lighter than it appears on spool. When basting, it is preferable to use a contrasting color, so that thread can be easily seen when unwanted stitches are removed. Always cut thread on an angle for easy insertion through needle eye. THREAD TYPES: 1. *Button and/or carpet thread*: extra strong, very durable. 2. *Buttonhole twist*: a silk thread which comes on small spools. Generally used for hand-worked buttonholes, decorative stitches, and sewing on buttons, it is stronger than cotton, making it easier to slip through fabric. 3. *Clear nylon thread*: strong, no-color thread, blends with any color fabric; used for hems, facings, etc. 4. *Elastic thread*: used for gathering by machine or hand. When machine-stitching use only on bobbin, stretching thread around bobbin. 5. *Embroidery floss*: six-strand twists of thread used for embroidery. May be separated into smaller strands, as needed. 6. *Mercerized cotton thread*: for general sewing on cotton, linen, rayon and cotton blends. 7. *Quilting thread*: for quilted articles; very strong. 8. *Silk thread*: used on fine woolens and silks. Does not leave marks on fabrics when removed. Excellent for bastings on tailored garments and produces a finer stitch. 9. *Synthetic thread* (polyester): for synthetic fabrics, knits, and their blends; strong, most often used.

THREAD COUNT

The number of threads in one square inch of fabric. The amount of the thread count is usually designated on packages of sheets and pillowcases. The greater the number of threads, the firmer and stronger the fabric.

THROAT PLATE

A metal plate directly under pressure foot on sewing machine, which has an opening for needle to pass through when stitching. Most sewing machines have markings ⅛″ apart as a guide for stitching seam widths accurately. A general throat plate has a wide opening accommodating any straight or zigzag stitching. It must be used with a general purpose foot. A small hole throat plate used with the straight stitch foot is excellent for preventing skipped stitches.

TIE DYE

Method of adding color designs to fabric by tying off areas of fabric before dipping into dye bath, thus preventing the color from entering those tied areas.

TISSUE PAPER

Thin, unlined paper used for adjusting patterns and transferring designs.

TODDLER

See FIGURE TYPE. Pattern size, which ranges from ½ yr. to 4 yrs. Patterns have diaper allowance, and dresses are shorter than "Girl" sizes. Measurements should be taken around body, across chest, and the height, to determine correct size.

TOP STITCHING

A line of stitching parallel to a seamline or finished edge; done on the right side of garment.

TRACING PAPER/DRESSMAKER'S CARBON

A form of carbon paper used with a tracing wheel to transfer construction markings from pattern to fabric. Comes in several colors. Choose a color close to that of fabric or white and be sure to place waxy surface against the wrong side of fabric.

TRACING WHEEL

A small, revolving wheel with a handle, used with tracing paper to mark pleats, darts, etc. Several types are available, some with a serrated edge and some with a smooth edge. Can be used on most fabrics.

TRAIN

Extension of garment which trails at back, usually on wedding dresses.

TRANSFER PATTERN

A pattern having stamped design printed on paper which can be transferred to fabric by ironing and is used as a guide for hand or machine embroidery.

TRANSPARENT TAPE

A see-through plastic stick-on tape purchased at stationery counters. Helpful in preparing patterns for adjustments, as a topstitching guide, for mending patterns, and for taping patterns in place when cutting pile fabrics and leather.

TRAPUNTO

A raised design used in quilting, by filling stitched design with batting.

TRICOT

Warp-knit fabric, highly run-resistant, it has very little lengthwise stretch. Characterized by vertical wales on the face of fabric and crosswise ribs on the back. Almost always used for linings in knit swimsuits and for undergarments.

TRIM

To cut away part of seam allowance after the seam has been stitched; to reduce bulk in an area.

TRIMMING

Decorative strips added to garment, such as rick-rack, braid or ribbon. Also referred to as "trim."

TROUSER CURTAIN

Durable fabric that extends below the inside waistband of trousers, keeping waist area from stretching. Holds pleats and seams in place and conceals stitching on interior of trousers.

TROUSERS

See PANTS.

TRUE GRAIN

See GRAIN.

T-SQUARE

A measuring device shaped like the letter "T." Made of plastic or metal. It is used for straightening grain lines, altering patterns, locating balance lines, and other markings.

TUBING

See CORDED TUBING.

TUBULAR KNIT

Fabric knitted in tubular form on circular machines. Excellent when using patterns requiring center front and center back sections to be placed on fold. One fold may be cut open and used as regular knit fabric.

TUCK

A stitched-down pleat used for fit or decoration. May be stitched down on the outside or on the inside of garment. Tiny tucks are called "pin-tucks."

TUCKER

See SEWING MACHINE ACCESSORY. Specially designed machine accessory enabling the sewer to achieve accurate widths of tucks by adjusting a numbered guide.

TULLE

Fine machine-made net fabric of silk, cotton, or synthetic fibers; used for bridal veils and ballet costumes.

TUNIC

Long top garment, to be worn over another garment.

TURTLENECK

A type of neckline with one-piece standing collar that folds down over itself covering the seamline. When using woven fabric, the collar section is cut on the bias; when using knits it is cut across the width of the fabric.

TWEED

A rough-textured, sturdy fabric with colorful spots or slubs; made of wool and blends.

TWEEZERS

Handy gadget with two prongs for removing tailor tacks, basting threads, etc.; sold at cosmetic counters.

TWILL TAPE

A narrow, extra-strong woven strip of cotton or polyester used as a stay to reinforce seams, for drawstrings or ties; used on roll-line of lapel when tailoring.

TWILL WEAVE

A basic weave of fabric in which the yarns interlace, creating a diagonal rib, usually running upward from left to right. Another twill weave has a chevron effect, zigzag in appearance, and is called herringbone twill.

U

UNBALANCED PLAID

See UNEVEN PLAID.

UNDERCOLLAR

Fabric that is joined to collar to form underside of collar. In ladies' wear it is usually of the same fabric; in men's wear it is frequently of melton cloth. Guide sheets sometimes refer to undercollar as "collar facing."

UNDERLAP

The part of a garment that extends under another part.

UNDERLAY

A shaped, additional piece of fabric placed under a section and stitched in place; seen on pleats and slot seams.

UNDERLINING

Fabric, lighter in weight than the outer fabric of a garment, cut exactly as the outer fabric and added to garment for support and to prevent stretching or sagging. It is basted to outer fabric and sewn together as one. Sometimes called "mounting."

UNDERSTITCHING

A row of machine stitching through the seam allowance, on right side of a facing, close to the seamline. This prevents the facing from rolling to the outside of garment.

UNEVEN BASTING

Temporary stitch used to attach interfacings or on areas where there is little or no strain, and a guide line for stitching seams, darts, pockets, etc. Stitches are done by hand, taking a long stitch on one side and a short stitch on the other side.

UNEVEN PLAID/UNBALANCED PLAID

A plaid design in which the pattern on both sides of the outstanding stripe is different. It may be different up and down, left to right, or in both directions.

UNIT CONSTRUCTION

The preparing and sewing of an entire section of garment before joining it to another.

UPPER COLLAR

The top or exposed part of a finished collar having two or more layers of fabric.

V

VELCRO

See NYLON CLOSURE TAPE.

VELOUR

Soft, closely woven fabric with a short, thick pile surface. Can be knitted or woven, and is usually made of cotton, wool, or mohair.

VELVET

Short, closely woven, cut pile fabric with a plain or twill weave on underside, it may be of silk or nylon. Luxurious hand, i.e., feel and drape.

VELVET BOARD

See NEEDLE BOARD.

VELVETEEN

Fabric with short, close filling, cut pile, usually of cotton, resembling velvet.

VENT

A slit or opening in a garment allowing the wearer more ease when walking or bending. This area is usually faced or lined.

VERTICAL

Construction lines going up and down on the body of a garment.

VEST

A short, sleeveless jacket, fitted to body curves, with buttons or other closures.

VICUNA

Fabric made from the wool of the vicuña llama, or a substitute, usually twilled and with a soft nap.

VOILE

Thin, transparent cloth, similar to organdy, but less stiff, with good draping qualities; tends to cling to body.

V-NECK

A shaped, front neckline in the form of the letter "V."

W

WADDING

See BATTING.

WAIST

Body measurement taken around the body at waistline; used for determining figure type.

WAISTBAND INTERFACING

A sturdy strip of canvas-type fabric used for reinforcement and to prevent waistband from rolling down.

WAISTLINE

Line of seam joining bodice and skirt at waist.

WAIST TO FLOOR

Body measurement taken from the side of the waist to the floor; used when constructing pants, evening gowns and long skirts. This measurement includes the turned-up hem.

WALES

Lengthwise loops in knitted fabrics. Also, the raised cords in woven fabric, e.g., corduroy.

WARP

Yarns running lengthwise in a woven fabric.

WARP KNITS

Knitted fabrics which have more stretch in their width than in their length.

WASH AND WEAR

Fabrics that can be washed and worn with little or no ironing.

WATER REPELLENT

Fabrics treated to prevent the absorption of water.

WEAVE

Process in which strands of thread or yarn are interlaced to make a fabric, on looms, by machines, or by hand. Plain weaves are interlaced in a fine, checkerboard fashion.

WEFT

See WOOF.

WELT

A strip of material applied decoratively to seam or edge; seen on pockets.

WELT POCKET

An inside pocket with opening on outside finished with a horizontal strip of self fabric.

WELTING

Fabric-covered cording having seam allowance exposed. Can be sewn into seams for decoration or reinforcement; seen on slipcovers and pillows.

WELT SEAM

A normal seam in which both seam allowances are pressed to one side, then topstitched parallel to seamline.

WHIPPING STITCH

See FELLING.

WIDTH

A horizontal direction.

WIGAN

Durable, loosely woven interfacing fabric, used around sleeve bottoms of tailored garments to reinforce hem. Hair canvas or other lightweight interfacings may also be used for this purpose.

WITH NAP

Fabrics with napped weave or one-way design; a cutting layout indicating how pattern is to be placed on fabric. Pattern should be laid and cut in one direction to prevent shading or design change. Pattern envelope indicates extra yardage needed for "with nap" fabrics.

WITHOUT NAP

Fabrics that do not have a pile, nap, or one-way design.

WOMEN

See FIGURE TYPE. A pattern selection for the fully mature figure. Larger than "Miss" and with longer back waist length.

WOOF or WEFT

Crosswise threads in a woven fabric or cross rows of loops in knit fabrics. Also called "filler."

WOOLEN

Yarns and fabrics that are made from short, natural animal fibers. These fabrics are resilient, warm, and durable, and are used primarily for outer garments and sweaters.

146

WOOL INTERFACINGS

See CANVAS.

WORK IN

To stretch fabric slightly while fitting it into a larger area.

WORSTED

A fabric woven from highly twisted, choice wool fibers which are smooth, strong, and firm, and which is excellent for tailoring.

WRAP-AROUND

A garment, or part of a garment, which wraps around the body, such as a skirt or cape, and which is held together with fasteners or self-fabric ties.

WRONG SIDE

The inside, or side of fabric that is undesirable for use on the outside of a garment.

Y

YARDAGE

1. The amount of fabric in a bolt. 2. The amount of fabric indicated on pattern envelope that will be needed to make a garment.

YARDSTICK

A measuring device, 36″ long with a flat surface and numbered markings, made of metal or wood. When purchasing a wood yardstick, be sure it has metal finished ends which will prevent warping. This is excellent for measuring lengths of fabric.

YARN

Continuous strands of fibers used in knitting, crocheting, weaving fabric, and the making of thread.

YARN DYEING

The coloring of yarn before it is woven or knitted.

YOKE

A garment section that crosses shoulder, joining back or front bodice, sometimes with gathers or pleats; also seen on hip area.

YOUNG JUNIOR TEEN

See FIGURE TYPE. A pattern selection for the just-developing teenage figure between 5′1″ and 5′3″ tall.

Z

ZIGZAG

A machine stitch where needle moves from left to right as it is stitching. A special throat plate and foot with wider opening is required. Small zigzag stitches may be used on knit fabrics to prevent seams from breaking. Also used as a seam finish on fabrics that ravel, by stitching close to edge, and used for appliqués, mending, or decoratively.

ZIPPER

A sliding fastener in use since 1891. This closure has metal or nylon teeth or coils which either close together, or open, when an attached pull-tab is raised or lowered. Available in a wide range of colors, lengths and weights. There are several types: *invisible*: when closed, this zipper appears as a continuous seamline, with the small pull-tab at the top; *conventional or neck zipper*: used when desiring an exposed, center or lapped application; *special purpose*: for specific functions, e.g., "separating" zipper, which is used to open and close jackets, coats, etc.

ZIPPER FOOT

See SEWING MACHINE ACCESSORY. A sewing machine accessory with one extended toe used in stitching close to a raised edge. The foot is adjustable to either the left or the right of the needle. Used for corded seams or for zipper insertion. *See also* INVISIBLE ZIPPER FOOT.

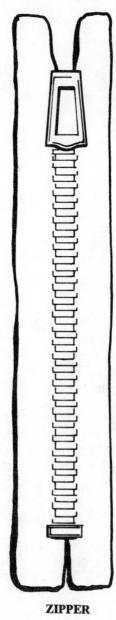

ZIPPER

150

ZIPPER PLACEMENT

A symbol on a pattern piece indicating placement of zipper on seamline for the required length of the zipper.

ZIPPER SHIELD

A narrow strip of interfaced fabric which is sewn along the length of a zipper on the inside of garment.

EQUIVALENCY CHART

CONVERTING INCHES TO CENTIMETERS AND YARDS TO METERS

This chart gives the standard equivalents as approved by the Pattern Fashion Industry.

mm — millimeters   **cm — centimeters**   **m — meters**

INCHES INTO MILLIMETERS AND CENTIMETERS
(Slightly rounded for your convenience)

inches	mm		cm	inches	cm
⅛	3mm			19	48.5
¼	6mm			20	51
⅜	10mm	or	1cm	21	53.5
½	13mm	or	1.3cm	22	56
⅝	15mm	or	1.5cm	23	58.5
¾	20mm	or	2cm	24	61
⅞	22mm	or	2.2cm	25	63.5
1	25mm	or	2.5cm	26	66
1¼	32mm	or	3.2cm	27	68.5
1½	38mm	or	3.8cm	28	71
1¾	45mm	or	4.5cm	29	73.5
2	50mm	or	5cm	30	76
2½	65mm	or	6.5cm	31	79
3	75mm	or	7.5cm	32	81.5
3½	90mm	or	9cm	33	84
4	100mm	or	10cm	34	86.5
4½	115mm	or	11.5cm	35	89
5	125mm	or	12.5cm	36	91.5
5½	140mm	or	14cm	37	94
6	150mm	or	15cm	38	96.5

EQUIVALENCY CHART

inches	mm	cm	inches	cm
7		18	39	99
8		20.5	40	101.5
9		23	41	104
10		25.5	42	106.5
11		28	43	109
12		30.5	44	112
13		33	45	114.5
14		35.5	46	117
15		38	47	119.5
16		40.5	48	122
17		43	49	124.5
18		46	50	127

YARDS TO METERS
(Slightly rounded for your convenience)

yards	meters	yards	meters	yards	meters	yards	meters	yards	meters
⅛	0.15	2⅛	1.95	4⅛	3.80	6⅛	5.60	8⅛	7.45
¼	0.25	2¼	2.10	4¼	3.90	6¼	5.75	8¼	7.55
⅜	0.35	2⅜	2.20	4⅜	4.00	6⅜	5.85	8⅜	7.70
½	0.50	2½	2.30	4½	4.15	6½	5.95	8½	7.80
⅝	0.60	2⅝	2.40	4⅝	4.25	6⅝	6.10	8⅝	7.90
¾	0.70	2¾	2.55	4¾	4.35	6¾	6.20	8¾	8.00
⅞	0.80	2⅞	2.65	4⅞	4.50	6⅞	6.30	8⅞	8.15
1	0.95	3	2.75	5	4.60	7	6.40	9	8.25
1⅛	1.05	3⅛	2.90	5⅛	4.70	7⅛	6.55	9⅛	8.35
1¼	1.15	3¼	3.00	5¼	4.80	7¼	6.65	9¼	8.50
1⅜	1.30	3⅜	3.10	5⅜	4.95	7⅜	6.75	9⅜	8.60
1½	1.40	3½	3.20	5½	5.05	7½	6.90	9½	8.70
1⅝	1.50	3⅝	3.35	5⅝	5.15	7⅝	7.00	9⅝	8.80
1¾	1.60	3¾	3.45	5¾	5.30	7¾	7.10	9¾	8.95
1⅞	1.75	3⅞	3.55	5⅞	5.40	7⅞	7.20	9⅞	9.05
2	1.85	4	3.70	6	5.50	8	7.35	10	9.15

AVAILABLE FABRIC WIDTHS

25″	65cm
27″	70cm
35″/36″	90cm
39″	100cm
44″/45″	115cm
48″	120cm
50″	127cm
54″/56″	140cm
58″/60″	150cm
68″/70″	175cm
72″	180cm

AVAILABLE ZIPPER LENGTHS

4″	10cm
5″	12cm
6″	15cm
7″	18cm
8″	20cm
9″	22cm
10″	25cm
12″	30cm
14″	35cm
16″	40cm
18″	45cm
20″	50cm
22″	55cm
24″	60cm
26″	65cm
28″	70cm
30″	75cm